DEMONS in Disguise

Fred DeRuvo

STUDY • GROW • KNOW
It's always time to study, grow and know your faith!

www.studygrowknow.com

Published in Scotts Valley, California, by Study-Grow-Know
www.studygrowknow.com • www.rightly-dividing.com • www.adroitpublications.com

Scripture quotations unless otherwise noted, are from The Holy Bible, King James Version. This version is in the public domain.

Images used in this publication (unless otherwise noted) are from clipartconnection.com and used with permission, ©2007 JUPITERIMAGES, and its licensors. All rights reserved.

All Woodcuts used herein are in the Public Domain and free of copyright.

All Figure illustrations used in this book were created by the author and protected under copyright laws, © 2010.

Parts of this book were previously published (though modified and edited for this book) from another one of the author's books, *Some of Satan's Major Lies Seen as Truth,* copyright 2009

Cover Design: Fred DeRuvo

Library of Congress Cataloging-in-Publication Data

DeRuvo, Fred, 1957 –

ISBN 0982644396
EAN-13 9780982644393

1. Religion – Demonology & Satanism

Contents

For such are false apostles, deceitful workers, transforming themselves into the apostles of Christ. And no marvel; for Satan himself is transformed into an angel of light. Therefore it is no great thing if his ministers also be transformed as the ministers of righteousness; whose end shall be according to their works.

– 2 Corinthians 11:13-15 (KJV)

FOREWORD

I have been studying and researching the area of aliens, the Nephilim, and Genesis 6 for some time. It's always been an interest of mine, because I was curious how aliens (if they exist *as* authentic beings from another planet and/or galaxy) possibly tie in with Scripture. To me, it always seemed as though aliens were mutually exclusive with the God of the Bible. The concept simply did not seem to fit.

When I first began pursuing information in this area, I was a very young Christian – around the age of 16 or so. I had only been a Christian for a few years, and my curiosity seemed to compel me to search for answers. Certainly, I searched the Bible, but in reality, the Bible seems to be quiet on certain areas, providing only a hint or two here and there about some subjects. I picked up a few books on the subject, but these seemed to provide answers that appeared to me to be extremely far-fetched.

I wanted to know what these beings were that others had claimed to have contact with, and I wanted to know from where they came. Were they simply figments of people's overactive imaginations? Were they real aliens, existing on their own planet far, far away from earth? If so, why did they bother coming here at all?

One night, I decided to do some soul searching under the stars. At that time, I lived just outside of Binghamton, NY, which was mainly rural. It was quiet, the sky was large, and the stars were bright. In fact, over the past week, there had been numerous sightings of shooting stars and other things in the skies. I thought this would be a good time to see what I could see. Behind our house was a hill that gently sloped upwards. I walked through the trees and brush eventually finding a suitable area. It was open enough to see a good portion of the sky, so there I sat, staring up into the night sky.

It was beautiful and peaceful. In fact, I started my "space watching" session really enjoying the solitude. After a short while, I saw one shooting star and then another in quick succession. This was very interesting and I was anxious to see more. I felt I had chosen a good night to check out the sky and wait for things to happen.

Interestingly enough, and for no reason that I noticed, it was not long before the tone of the situation became a bit *dark* and I'm not referring to the sky itself, which was already plenty dark, lit only by light reflecting off stars. I have no idea why I began to sense something wrong, but there it was and I could not shake it. The longer I sat there, the more pronounced it became. I searched myself and could not figure out what was going on because I knew I was not afraid of any aliens (though maybe I should have been). I was not afraid of the dark or of the field where I sat. I was too familiar with this area to be afraid of it.

Yet, the longer I sat, the worse the sense of foreboding became and all I could say was that it was very weird, and unlike me. Finally, I got the sense that what I was waiting for to appear was *evil*, *malevolent*. I have no idea why I began to sense this about the situation. Who knows, but maybe a few of the books I had read stating that these beings were nothing more than demons began to play on my mind. Whatever the case, I decided I had done enough sky watching for one night and hurried back to the house, feeling a bit like a chicken.

In the interim years between that incident and today, over 35 years have passed. I like to think that I have gained a greater insight into the entire alien phenomenon. In fact, what I have noticed is that compared to the early 1970s, a great many books have been written on this subject. Some of it has come from well-known individuals within the New Age movement. Individuals who are not particularly religious in any sense have written other books. There have also been a many books written by Christian authors who have also studied this phenomenon for many years and have shared their findings. To these individuals, I am grateful. I am grateful for their dedication, their work, and their follow through in putting their thoughts and findings down on paper in book format. To these people, this book is dedicated, people like L. A. Marzulli, Stephen Quayle, Chuck Missler, Tom Horn, Patrick Heron, and many others too numerous to mention here – thank you.

This particular book is one that has been a long time coming and the time is right for it now. After reading many of the books published, I believe there is really only one conclusion to arrive at if one is a Christian. At the same time, there is at least one question that has not been answered and really cannot be answered dogmatically. I tackle that question in this book.

Fred DeRuvo, March 2010

Chapter 1

Guess Who?

Aliens have been a hot topic for some time as most of us are aware. In fact, even before Roswell, people claimed either to have *seen* a UFO, or been *abducted* by space beings on UFOs. Jacques Vallee mentions that throughout history, there have actually been more UFO/alien sightings *before* our modern day, than *during* our modern day.[1]

Since the Roswell incident, the amount of sightings and claims of abductions have risen astronomically (no pun intended). Now, in

---

[1] Jacques Vallee, *Confrontations* (Ballantine Books: New York 1990), 162

2010, talk of extraterrestrials, aliens, beings from other planets, intelligent forms of life, or whatever else they are called is considered a *normal* conversation. Very few (except the diehard skeptic) really question the topic anymore. What most people disagree about is *who* or *what* these beings actually are, not *if* they exist or not. While there are groups of individuals who do not accept the reality of ET existence, these now seem to be in the minority to be sure. At least it would seem so. Even some atheists are starting to think in terms of "higher powers" or other intelligent life forms elsewhere in our universe.

Are They Real or Not?

It should not come as a surprise when considering the entire alien phenomenon, opinions range from they *do not exist*, to they *are demons*, or to the belief that they are who they appear to be; *intelligent beings* from other places. Certainly, each reader of this book has an opinion as well, or at least an interest, else there would be little reason to be reading this book right now.

For years, I teetered back and forth about whether these being actually existed and if so, were they *demons* or authentic *aliens*? In fact, I remember reading books that stated the events in Ezekiel for instance (the wheel in the sky, etc.), were nothing more than aliens who traveled long distances to arrive on this planet.

For those authors who thought like that, the Bible seemed to confirm to them that aliens *did* exist and the Bible *proved* it. They did not consider the fact that what they read in the book of Ezekiel and elsewhere was actually what Ezekiel *saw*, which was God in His *glory*, along with certain angelic hosts.

In my mind, the alien beings that have become part of the fabric of society throughout the world today fall into two categories. Either they are:

1. *Authentic extraterrestrials who have and continue to visit this planet,* or
2. *Demons, disguising themselves as extraterrestrials who have and continue to visit this planet*

In either case, we know that these beings are not merely here *sightseeing,* or on *vacation.* At the same time, it is obvious that determining *who* they are is only *half* the battle. *Why* they have come and *continue* to come to earth is another problem altogether, but may be understood by discovering *why* they continue to visit this planet at all.

If these beings fall into the first category noted above – *authentic extraterrestrials* – we *still* need to determine the reason for their visitation. The same applies to the second category, though it obviously becomes more obvious. As we endeavor to determine the truth of their mission, I believe that their *identity* becomes *plain.*

Deceiving is Their Nature

Most people, who are not "religious," do not normally see past the fact that these beings do *exist,* though not as what they may *believe.* In other words, from the books I have read on the subject by Dr. Jacques Vallee, Dr. David Jacobs and numerous others (who do not seem to display a belief in the supernatural, in the Judeo-Christian sense), they usually end up seeing these beings as aliens with evil intentions, or as *malevolent.* While they tend to believe that these are actual aliens or some form of ET from other planetary systems, they are concerned that their mission to earth seems to be one in which we should *fear.*

In the case of Vallee, he has concluded that these beings are actually *inter-dimensional,* as opposed to *extraterrestrial.* If so, then this would also explain a number of things to us, such as how *quickly* they can appear and disappear into and from our system.

Others – normally those involved in some aspect of the New Age movement – do *not* question the actual existence of extraterrestrials (or "Ascended Masters") from other planets. They see these beings altruistically, here to *help* to earth and its citizens. They believe these outer space beings not only come in *peace*, but come to help us *achieve* greater things, in order that our planet and we will *evolve* to the next level of our supposed pre-planned existence.

Most Christians whose books I have read believe that these beings are nothing more than *demons*. These demons, in collusion with, and under the watchful eye of fallen angels and Satan, have created this complex masquerade allowing them to communicate with many individuals on earth. Their communications (or *transmissions*), tell of an alien mandate to help our fledgling planet, so that we will not wind up destroying ourselves.

I am convinced, along with many others, that these beings are in fact *demons*, clothed with intricate disguises that not only *mask* their actual *identity*, but their true *purposes* as well. It is important for us to sift through the research and material available to us. While doing so, we need to take seriously the messages allegedly received by human beings on this planet from these space beings. What is the *content* of these various transmissions? Is it one of *peace*, or *threat*? Is there a way to know beyond doubt? Do we need to read between the lines of these alien communications, in order to get a better picture of their intent?

Not only are these ETs *not* going away, but they also seem to be revealing themselves in greater numbers and frequency, in both *physicality* and *communication*. In essence, they have become *braver* in stepping up the occurrence of *incidental* contact, human *abduction*, cattle *mutilation*, as well as revealing their squadron of ships in the sky. They do not merely appear and then vanish in all instances. In many cases, one UFO, or an entire fleet will appear and remain in the sky long enough for many people to grab their still or video cameras and record the event.

All of this says a great deal about them *and* their willingness to be seen in the open. In fact, it appears as if they *want* us to notice them and interact with humans. What has *changed*? What is *now* causing them to seemingly toss apprehension to the wind? Why *now*? More importantly, if they *have* stepped up the frequency of their visitations, why have they not actually stopped to *introduce* themselves and speak to *all* of us, or at least the leaders of our countries?

Was Roswell the Beginning?

If *aliens* have been with us since at least 1947 (and probably much earlier), then one can only wonder why they have taken so long to get to this point of being *unafraid* (if that's the right word) to reveal themselves, yet they still hold back. It is almost as if they are now *teasing* us, wanting us to *want* them to come out into the open. Certainly, if the hints we have seen throughout history are considered, then it is very possible that aliens in some form have been with us since the days of ancient Egypt and before.

Something though, has kept them in the shadows. Something has barred them from revealing themselves all at once to a world, which *they* believe (and state) apparently *needs* them. Are they waiting to see whether we would "evolve" to a higher plane all by ourselves? Are they remaining in the shadows until such a time as they feel they *must* reveal and help us because we are unable to help ourselves?

Have they finally accepted the notion that we need their *intellect*, their *expertise*, their *technology*, and maybe everything else they offer? On the other hand, are they all playing one huge *trick* on us *as demons in disguise*? If that is the case, then it is clear that the subject of aliens and all that goes with it, is *phony*, merely a smokescreen to prevent us from understanding their *true* purpose.

Chapter 2

The Actual Possibilities

There are many places we can begin in our search for answers. In this book, I have specifically chosen *not* to spend a good amount of time going over the possible *origins* of these beings. Simply an introduction of the subject will do, drawing on the work of others. Convinced that these space aliens are nothing but Nephilim demons and fallen angels, the majority of this book will focus on *why* these particular entities are doing what they are doing, *how* they are making it happen, and *what* they hope to accomplish. There may well be a follow up book as the subject is so varied.

Volumes have been written on the subject, and one of the best places to start in my opinion is with Stephen Quayle. My first introduction to Quayle was through his book *Giants*, which is the result of over 30 years of research on Genesis 6:4. His studies take us back to the beginning, at least to the beginning of *human* history.

"There were giants in the earth in those days; and also after that, when the sons of God came in unto the daughters of men, and they bare children to them, the same became mighty men which were of old, men of renown," (KJV).

Quayle Weighs In

Quayle's book provides what I believe to be tremendous insight into the *ramifications* of this particular verse. In essence, he believes that these "mighty men" were certainly that, *mighty*, but they were also *far* more than *simply* mighty *men*. Quayle takes the position that they were mighty men because of an interbreeding between *fallen angels* and *human women*. Moreover, he indicates a connection between these mighty men and *giants*. In fact, it is difficult to come away from a serious study of this text without understanding that these mighty men were literal *giants* of abnormal *size, strength, agility, prowess,* and *intelligence.*

Quayle's book offers information on the many *overgrown* human skeletons that have been unearthed over the centuries. Some of these skeletons measured eight feet, 12 feet, and over 20 feet in height! This is nothing to shrug off, though it is difficult to believe. If humans (or creatures that *appeared* human) existed at these heights, it needs to be seriously considered and the reason *why* needs to be determined.

If these individuals actually grew to heights of 12, 15, 23, 25, or more feet tall, then *something* obviously happened to cause that to occur, since there is nothing in Scripture that indicates Adam and Eve were that tall. What was it? While some believe these oversized beings stem from the fallen line of *Seth*, I do not share that belief. For Quayle and many other researchers, it all goes back to Genesis 6 and the concept that these mighty men were in fact, *giants of old*. These *men of renown* were the men that the Greeks wrote about in what we view today as *myths*. We think of the Titans or gods like Zeus, Hermes, and others, and we believe them to be products of extremely creative human minds and nothing more. In our modern world, we do not consider them to have been *real* individuals by any stretch. The Iliad and the Odyssey, as well as other adventures of Greek lore are just that to most of us, *Greek lore*, but are they?

G. H. Pember notes *"May there not be great significance in the fact that the very name of Satan passes, through its Chaldaic form 'Sheitan,' in the Greek 'Titan,' which the last word is used by Greek and Latin poets as a designation of the Sun-god."*[2]

Genesis 6:4 hardly stands out to the average reader. In fact, if you read the verse quickly, the only thing that might catch your attention is the phrase *"mighty men which were of old."* At first glance, that could actually mean a number of things.

It *could* mean that some men were simply more powerful than others were. They may have been more powerful *physically*, or *mentally*, or both. It could also mean that there was a certain lore or myth attached to some of these men, which grew as time progressed, becoming larger than the men themselves. These myths became the stuff of lore and carried from one generation to the next, increasing slightly with every new telling.

Quayle states that the English translation of this verse tends to *obscure* the real meaning. That is no surprise since it is often difficult to translate meaning precisely when going from one language to another. English itself is not the easiest language in the world to

---

[2] G. H. Pember, *Earth's Earliest Ages* (Suffolk: Kessinger, 1942), 38

learn or to translate into, because of all the nuances, the figures of speech, the multiple meanings of most words and more.

Quayle believes (as do many Bible scholars and I concur as well), that these mighty men were *more* than simply *human* men who had greater intellect or displayed additional physical prowess. He traces the entire key to understanding this subject to *Satan* himself.

It's All Part of Satan's Plan

We are all aware (or should be) of *how* and *why* Satan fell from grace. Initially he was the anointed cherub, the one who oversaw all angelic beings, and yet in spite of all that he was and all that he had control over, it was not good enough for him. We have no idea how long it took, but eventually for Satan (who was Lucifer before his fall) pride sprang up within his heart. We see the record of this in both Isaiah 14 and Ezekiel 28. Here again, scholars of the Bible disagree over these references and whether they refer to Satan or not. It seems clear enough that either the verses in both cases are highly *poetic*, or they are literal, referencing an individual who is much more than merely human.

When pride *was* found within Satan's heart, he fell from his first estate. In the process, he managed to convince one third of the angelic host to follow him in his rebellion against God. These angels became *fallen* like him because they too literally fell from the estate to which God had created them.

Book of Enoch

Even though it is understood that the *Book of Enoch* is not a divinely inspired work, nonetheless, it contains helpful information about these fallen angels and their Nephilim offspring. This information *potentially* serves to bring more of this mystery into the open. It would seem that these fallen angels were originally called *Watchers* in the *Book of Enoch*.

Sent by God, the Watchers' instructions were to *watch* over the earth. Apparently, these 200 Watchers began to *lust* after human women. They fell into sin when they followed their lust, entering into sexual unions with these women. The sense we get from Genesis is that these men *took* (forcefully) as many women as they wanted to have for themselves. A hybrid offspring was the result (cf. Enoch 6:1-2; 7:1-6). The corruption of the human genetic code had *begun*.

The *Book of Enoch* indicates that as the offspring (Nephilim) physically died, their spirits continued to exist. They *were* the evil spirits, destined to roam the earth until judged. They spend their time harassing and oppressing humanity. Another book which bears testimony to this is the *Book of Jubilees*, which as Missler states confirms that the beings referred to as demons in the New Testament, are the same *"disembodied spirits of the Nephilim."*[3]

However, does *Scripture teach, suggest,* or *imply* this? Do we *know* of a time when this may have taken place in which the Bible itself tells us of these things?

In Genesis 6:1-2, we read, *"And it came to pass, when **men** began to multiply on the face of the earth, and daughters were born unto them, that the **sons of God** saw the daughters of men that they were fair; and they took them wives of all which they chose."* (emphasis added)

In the first part of the text, the noun *"men"* is used to refer to *human* men, who began to multiply and had daughters (of men). The *next* section uses the phrase *sons of God*. Why the switch? Why go from referring to men as *men*, to men as *sons of God*? The only logical conclusion is that the writer of Genesis, under the direct inspiration of God, used the phrase *sons of God*, because he was referring *not* to human men at that point, but to *angelic* males. If not, there is really no need to use two different references in the same section of

---

[3] Chuck Missler, *Alien Encounters* (Coeur d'Alene: Koinonia House 1997), 206

Scripture if *both* refer to the same *type* of being, namely *human*. This use of *sons of God* is used in Job to signify angelic hosts (cf. Job 1:6).

We also know that both Peter and Jude quote from the *Book of Enoch*. It is interesting when we consider that if the *Book of Enoch* was available to these men, it was available to nearly everyone at that time, *including* of course Jesus Himself. There is no reason to believe that Jesus would *not* have read and studied the *Book of Enoch*. It is obvious that both Peter and Jude *did*, since they quote from it, and it is doubtful that they simply scanned the book looking for a choice verse or two to pull from it to include in their epistles. Undoubtedly, they were very familiar with the book and very possibly understood it as truth. In fact, there is no good reason to believe that they *doubted* the truthfulness of the book since they actually quoted from its contents.

Uninspired But Can Still Clarify

Even if the *Book of Enoch* is *not* inspired, the truth remains that if nothing else it can be viewed as we view commentaries or books of history today. I know of no commentary that is inspired as the Bible is inspired, yet that does *not* diminish the integrity or helpfulness of the commentary or history book itself. In fact, many commentaries provide wonderful insight into passages of Scripture that helps us in our biblical studies.

We view books that delve into the Hebrew or Greek in the same manner, as well as those that shed light on the culture of the time. These books are often invaluable as we seek to gain *God's meaning* from Scripture. There is nothing wrong with using these books at all, though we should not view them as equal to God's Word in authority. In fact, the person who uses *nothing* but the Bible might find himself or herself in a better position to embrace *error* here and there. They may take this approach because they have decided that *only* the Holy Spirit can teach them, and they need no one else.

Let's be clear in noting that the Holy Spirit *does* teach us, however, He *also* teaches us *through* those whom God has given to the Church in the form of pastors and teachers. Obviously, it is important for us to do as the Bereans did when they heard Paul preach and teach, but to automatically neglect or *negate* all human teachers solely because you believe that you should only go to the Holy Spirit is not only prideful, but discounts the *gifts* that God has given other individuals within the Body of Christ.

Quayle (along with Missler, Fruchtenbaum and others) makes a great case for the fact that quite possibly, prior to the Creation of the world, (or "renovation" of the world after cataclysmic destruction), a different system existed that God created. Unfortunately, it would also appear that something rather dramatic and devastating took place, destroying much of God's original creation. This dramatic event was undoubtedly the battle that took place between God and His angels and Satan along with his followers. The result of this confrontation was *chaos* and *void*, much like how a war torn area of the globe looks *after* the war. Destruction remains in its wake and the only thing left is to clean up and rebuild.

This is quite possibly why this verse states, "*And the earth was* **without form***, and* **void***; and darkness was upon the face of the deep. And the Spirit of God moved upon the face of the waters,*" (Genesis 1:1; emphasis added).

Possible Connection with Jeremiah?
Quayle looks to Jeremiah 4, equating the above verse with it. The verses he culls from Jeremiah read this way, "*I beheld the earth, and, lo, it was without form, and void; and the heavens, and they had no light. I beheld the mountains, and, lo, they trembled, and all the hills moved lightly. I beheld, and, lo, there was no man, and all the birds of the heavens were fled. I beheld, and, lo, the fruitful place was a wilderness, and all the cities thereof were broken down at the presence of the LORD, and by his fierce anger,*" (Jeremiah 4:23-26)

Quayle believes that many prophetic areas of Scripture occur numerous times in the Bible. He sees this as referring to the destruction that occurred prior to the creation of Adam, *as well as* pointing to the destruction of Jerusalem later on.

There may be some merit to this view, since the very first verse of Jeremiah 4 coincides with Genesis 1:1, with the words, "*I beheld the earth, and lo, it was without form, and void.*" There really has been no time other than just *before* the creation of Adam that the earth might have been described in this manner, at least that we know of. In fact, the *past* tense forms of the verbs in the text provide additional evidence pointing to that time in prehistory.

Verse 25 of Jeremiah 4 is also significant in that it points out that no human being *existed*. It would appear as though these verses describe something that went from being *fruitful* and *beautiful* to something that ends up being *desolate* and *ugly*. I believe Quayle makes some good points here.

If there *had* been a civilization before Adam, with ours beginning *with* the creation of Adam, it also means that some devastating clash occurred between powerful forces and beings. With the information we have gained regarding Satan's fall from grace, the fallen angels, and the verbiage of both Genesis 1:1 and the Jeremiah 4 passage, it would seem that a number of things have lined up that make sense.

The Gap Theory
While studying at Philadelphia College of Bible, we studied this same area of Scripture, labeled the *Gap Theory*. Many qualified Bible scholars have fallen and do fall on both sides of the issue, with some finding reasons to support it and others finding reasons to deny it. This is one of those areas in Scripture allowing individuals to make up his own mind. Finding support for or against in no way takes away from our *salvation*. It is one of the *non-essentials* of the faith. As Paul would say, we need to be convinced in our own minds. At the

same time, it is pointless and futile to enter into debates about biblical subjects like this, because these debates often quickly turn into *quarrels*, bringing *dishonor*, instead of *glory* to God.

Not long ago, I visited one website that had placed up a PowerPoint® with narration concerning the Nephilim of the Old Testament. The instructor had an interesting viewpoint about what the Nephilim were, but one with which I disagreed. After reading some of the comments, I posted my own *opinion*. I clearly acknowledged that I was presenting my *view*, not wanting to take the chance of someone thinking that I was coming down on his or her opinion, or presenting myself as a know-it-all on the subject.

Not long after my post, someone named Paul posted his own response to my initial post. It read in part, "*As far as the other comment above about Angels having the ability to reproduce but the (sic) don't by choice, that is ridiculous (sic). If we understand that God does everything for a purpose and to create angels and not allow them to reproduce (Marry or be given in marriage) makes no sense at all. Man was given the ability to procreate, for the purpose of populating the earth. Of Angels, the Word of God says in Hebrews 1:14 that ALL His angels are ministering spirits sent forth to minister for those who will inherit salvation.*"[4]

If someone chooses to disagree with me, that is fine. It should be obvious how his comments could have been presented much more charitably. We went back and forth a few times and I did my best to calmly present my view, emphasizing again that my view was my *opinion*.

Another of his responses was, "*Fred, speculation can turn into heresie (sic) very quickly, and a rule I learned a long time ago when it comes to the exposition of scripture, is where the scripture is silent, we should be*

---

[4] http://www.prophecywatch.com/video/slideshows/the-nephilim-fallen-angels-and-the-last-days/the-nephilim-fallen-angels-and-the-last-days-part-1

silent or tread with fear and trepidation. Many people have been lead (sic) away captive into false doctrine as a result of speculation and imaginative ideas, and that is the point where it can turn into damnable heresies as the scripture says (2 Peter 2:1). My suggestion is we take speculation with a grain of salt. It is not a matter of wrapping my brain around it, it is a matter of being verified, and clarified, by the scripture, and we as students of the word must be careful on what we teach or preach, especially on topics such as this one that can lead into a miriad (sic) of other false doctrines."[5]

Now Paul has gone from stating that my view is *ridiculous*, to one bordering on (or could lead to), *heresy*. The problem is that what we were discussing had nothing to do with *salvation*, or any of the other fundamentals of the faith.

In that sense then, the subject of aliens, Nephilim, or the Gap Theory could *never* be considered heresy, except to those who do not fully understand the meaning of the word as applied to biblical theology. If it somehow takes away from *salvation*, or exactly *Jesus* is, then yes. In its current form, regarding the subject we were discussing, *no*. It is merely a *belief* that neither adds nor takes away from my faith. It is an *interesting* area of study and that is basically it.

Blah, Blah, Blah

After I responded to his comments above, he stated in response, "*All I can do is reiterate that we must be careful when speculating about certain topics in the scripture. As I said, it CAN lead to heresy, I didn't say it would, I said it CAN. Having lived in a part of the world where Mormons are the predominant religion, pre-existing spirit babys (sic) are a part of their false doctrine, which also includes Another Jesus which is contrary to the Jesus of the bible. So I am on the defense when it comes to speculation. Nothing wrong with speculation, just as long as*

---

[5] http://www.prophecywatch.com/video/slideshows/the-nephilim-fallen-angels-and-the-last-days/the-nephilim-fallen-angels-and-the-last-days-part-1

we don't make a theology out of it. The gap theory is another highly disputed speculative idea. However once again, where the scripture is silent, we must be careful. Many people also use writings from the **Book of Enoch** *and others to feed their ideas, and these books are not canon and it can get peoples (sic) minds off on a wrong thinking mode, and for some, into Alice's rabbit hole. Regardless of how much learning we have acquired, we ALL are susceptible to error, because we are human."*[6] (emphasis added)

Paul is trying to clarify himself and convince that *he* is right, when in fact, only God *knows* the truth with respect to the Gap Theory. It is *not* supposed to be something people quarrel or divide over, nor is it to be something that becomes *dogma* for individuals. We can never really know this side of heaven, the truth about this subject. The best we can do is to arrive at conclusions based on the circumstantial evidence available to us. It does not matter if people agree or disagree over subjects like these. The thing that matters most is *how* people *treat* one another in the midst of disagreements.

Are Angels Genderless?

Even as I attempted to explain my view that while yes, Jesus said the angels are neither married nor given in marriage, I did not believe Jesus was necessarily saying that they have *no* ability to procreate if given the chance, or that they are somehow *genderless*. In saying that, I believe Jesus meant that when human beings die and go to heaven, they no longer have the *need* to procreate or marry, namely because we will be married to Jesus. He used the reference to the elect angels to support His point. We know from Scripture that Satan and his angels have a great deal of power and ability.

In *Giants*, Stephen Quayle spends a good amount of time discussing aspects of this *possible* Gap Theory. He also discusses what it may

---

[6] http://www.prophecywatch.com/video/slideshows/the-nephilim-fallen-angels-and-the-last-days/the-nephilim-fallen-angels-and-the-last-days-part-1

have meant for earth and the humans, which came afterwards. After laying that groundwork, he begins dealing with the subject of Genesis 1:1, the "*mighty men.*"

Quayle delves into the subject of *giants*, as they appear throughout history in mythology. As noted, we read of the Titans, Hercules, Zeus, Hermes, and other gods of the Greeks, with corresponding names in Roman context. Native American culture also contains mythology related to tall, red-haired giants who not only possessed exceptional strength and skill, but also were extremely fast runners, able to overtake a buffalo.

Regarding these myths, Quayle states, "*The greatest proof of the parallels between historic and biblical accounts of the past and those of various cultures' myths are to be found in cultures, which had written fables and religious stories. That these are similar affirms the idea that common ancestors and histories are to be found among most of the peoples of the world.*"[7]

Longwalkers

Quayle has another book out called, *Longwalkers*, which has an interesting cover. The designer who created the book's cover is said (by Quayle) to have created the scene from the description and crude drawing by one of the soldiers who was present and allegedly saw the beast. Quayle's book is actually a fictionalized screenplay involving a group of beasts like the one on the cover attempting to take over the world by waking up other creatures in suspended animation. What interested me more than anything was simply the *cover*, since it is based on an event that allegedly occurred. Quayle also includes the soldier's own account of the incident in the back of book.

---

[7] Stephen Quayle, *Giants* (Bozeman: End Time Thunder Publishers 4th printing, 2008), 61

The event took place on September 19, 2005 in Afghanistan. The soldier's job was to pilot his cargo plane in and out of the area, either bringing things *to* the other soldiers stationed in that area (known as the Soviet Valley of Death), or carry things out.

The pilot states that on one particular cargo mission, he and a crew of six were dispatched to the area to bring out some *cargo*. When they arrived, they learned that what they were going to be carting out was in fact, a *giant*; a *dead* giant.

The first thing the pilot noticed was the giant's size. It was overwhelmingly large. It was on a pallet, which he states was approximately 9 ft x 7.3 ft. Even at that, part of the giant's frame (though placed on it in a fetal position) extended *off* the pallet on both sides. The estimated weight of the giant was roughly 1500 pounds, and the probable height was 10-12 feet tall. After deducting the weight of the pallet, plastic and netting, the giant weighed in at approximately 1100 pounds.

The giant apparently had six fingers on the one hand that stuck out from under the plastic and netting. The pilot estimated the giant's feet at 30 inches in length. The smell was incredible. The pilot stated that the skin of the giant was very whitish, though certainly some of that could have been from the beginning stages of decomposition.

The way in which the military located the giant was interesting in and of itself. Apparently, a team of Marines was out hunting Taliban when they came across a small village. These villagers knew of the giant that lived in the caves *above* the village. The Marines believed that this "giant" was likely a Taliban extremist being protected by the villagers, so they went up to investigate. As they entered the mouth of the cave, they noticed remains of decapitated soldiers strewn around the cave. As soon as the giant noticed the intruders, he became extremely angry and ran toward them with a swiftness that was apparently unbelievably fast. The Marines took him out with their M-16s and AK-47s. Once they airlifted the body to Germany, the cargo was unloaded and that is the last the pilot ever heard or saw of it.[8] Did this event actually happen? No one can prove it, as there are no photos or videos of the creature.

Regarding these giants, Chuck Missler states, "*apparently these unnatural offspring, the Nephilim, were monstrous and they have been memorialized in the legends and myths of every ancient culture on the planet Earth...the Nephilim also seem to be echoed in the legendary Greek demigods. Throughout Greek mythology we find that intercourse between the gods and women yielded half-god, half-man Titans, demigods, or heroes which were partly terrestrial and partly celestial.*"[9]

While we should *not* necessarily view mythology as historical *truth*, we *can* gain from it an understanding of how different cultures viewed subjects like giants, or even Noah's Ark, and the global Flood. The viewpoints of these ancient civilizations are important to consider when doing any research like this, because of what *may* come to the surface.

Pre-Adamic Culture

"*Over the course of thirty years of investigation, I can safely say that I am convinced beyond a shadow of a doubt, that it is possible not only to learn much about this ancient pre-Adamic race, but also to see the remnants of their ancient cities.*"[10]

Quayle's above comment is indicative of the position that he has arrived at after doing years of research. Science has corroborated many avenues through research, especially in the form of ancient unearthed artifacts. Because of this and other discoveries, the inescapable conclusion for Quayle lies in the (alleged) fact that fallen

---

[8] Stephen Quayle & Duncan Long, *Longwalkers – The Return of the Nephilim*
[9] Chuck Missler, *Alien Encounters* (Coeur d'Alene: Koinonia House 1997), 240
[10] Stephen Quayle, *Giants* (Bozeman: End Time Thunder Publishers 4th printing, 2008), 81

angels *did* in fact co-mingle with human women, producing a hybrid race of angel/human *creatures*.

The sad fact of the matter is that many to most of these artifacts discovered throughout the decades and centuries, once unearthed seem to have disappeared. One cannot help but wonder what would happen if these unearthed discoveries were revealed to the public. The entire scientific world might very well be turned on its head! That is certainly a good enough reason for the evolutionary scientific community to want to keep these things out of public view.

For instance, what do you do with bones of human-type beings ranging in height between 12, 15, 23, or 28 feet? This information would certainly *negate* aspects of evolution, or the whole system of evolution altogether. How were the pyramids and other structures completed by ancient men? We have no *sure* way of knowing, even with our technology. While there have been some wonderful educated guesses, we do not understand unequivocally how Stone Henge came to be, how the statues on Easter Island got there, or how the pyramids came to fruition. They *were* obviously created though, and the way modern man is taught to believe ancient man existed, not only would they *not* have had the brainpower, but according to evolution, they lacked the skills and technology as well. Yet, there they stand, these structures, which defy current human wisdom and technology regarding their creation.

Could there have been giants on the earth? Could the mighty men of Genesis 1 have actually *been* gigantic human beings (on the outside), who came about as a product of fallen angels cohabitating with human women? If not that, then what were they? The only other answer would have to be *demons* or *devils*. A problem immediately rises to the surface though, and it can be found in Peter and Jude's quotes from the *Book of Enoch*. Let's take a moment to look at the texts.

Peter states, "*For if God spared not the **angels that sinned**, but cast them down to hell, and delivered them into chains of darkness, to be reserved unto judgment; And spared not the old world, but saved Noah the eighth person, a preacher of righteousness, bringing in the flood upon the world of the ungodly,*" (2 Peter 2:4, emphasis added).

Jude says, "*And the angels **which kept not their first estate, but left their own habitation**, he hath reserved in everlasting chains under darkness unto the judgment of the great day,*" (Jude 6, emphasis added).

In both cases above, we read of angels that *sinned*, or angels that did not keep their *first estate*. While some believe that this refers to *all* the angels that rebelled with Satan against God, it seems that this view cannot be accurate.

First, *if* the *entirety* of angels who rebelled with Satan is being referred to here, then *who* or *what* are the demons in the New Testament? If *all* fallen angels are currently kept in darkness, then the question of the *existence* of demons immediately comes to the fore, unless they happen to be *all* that remains of these entities for Satan's use.

However, *if* both Peter and Jude are referring to only *some* of the fallen angels, or even a specific group within the ranks of the fallen angels, then it makes much more sense. In this way, neither Peter nor Jude refer to *all* the angels, but a select *group* of them.

These particular angels did something so heinous that their punishment includes being chained in darkness until the Great White Throne Judgment. This means these *particular* angels are *not* free to roam around and harass anyone, much less God's children. This then cancels out the possibility that these angels are the demons of Christ's day *and* our day, since they are now in chains.

Semjaza Kicks Things Off

Determining exactly what both Peter and Jude are referring to within the *Book of Enoch* will provide us with insight into their meaning and understanding of the text. We have already pointed out that Enoch refers to a group of angels sent to earth by God to observe and protect. Enoch further states that this was a group of 200 angels, led by one particular angel named Semjaza (or Samyaza, depending upon your version of the *Book of Enoch*). In fact, according to the *Book of Enoch*, the whole scheme to take human wives was fully Semjaza's idea and he persuaded the other 199 Watchers to participate with him, He did not want to be the only one to take the blame.

"'Come, let us choose us wives from among the children of men and have children with them.' And Semjaza, who was their leader said to them, 'I fear you will not agree to do this deed and I alone shall have to pay the penalty of this great sin.' And they all answered him and said, 'Let us all swear an oath, and all bind ourselves by mutual curses so we will not abandon this plant but to do this thing'."[11]

The above scenario is most definitely interesting. If there is any truth at all there, it becomes clear that both Jude and Peter *believed* it to be the case; otherwise, it is highly doubtful that they would have incorporated any part of the *Book of Enoch* in their own letters, much less this part, unless they viewed it *allegorically*. However, the way the text is composed there is nothing there that would indicate either Peter or Jude referred to these chained angels in the *allegorical* sense.

---

[11] Joseph B. Lumpkin *Fallen Angels, the Watchers, and the Origins of Evil* (Fifth Estate: 2006), 55

Chapter 3

Aliens or Nephilim?

Real Alien or Nephilim Spirit?

There are really only *two* choices when it comes to the space *beings* that *seem* to be from other planets or galaxies. Either they are the real deal, *aliens* visiting us from other systems, or they are what have become known as Nephilim, *revisiting* us from times past. Each person will make their own decision based on what *they* read and how *they* view the information available to them.

People like Stephen Quayle, Chuck Missler and others have done us a tremendous service by providing Scriptural insight into the problem of Genesis 6:4, based on their own research. Both of them spend time dealing with the Hebrew word translated "giant." They discuss the ramifications of it. They believe the best scenario is to accept that these beings are the result of *fallen angels* co-mingling with *human women*. It is difficult to believe that these mighty men came about through the line human of Seth. It is hard to believe anything else, other than *some* fallen angels found a way to procreate with human women. The result was a monstrosity, a hybrid creature both human and angelic, and completely *fallen*.

One thing I also believe to be in favor of this view is that phrase, "*sons of God*," vs. "*daughters of men*." There is an obvious difference between these two groups and it is not *merely* in gender. The phrase "*sons of God*" is used only three times in Scripture and when it is used in the book of Job, it clearly corresponds with angels (cf. Job 1:6). I believe the same to be true with its use in Genesis 6, for reasons already noted.

A Hybrid Race

If the offspring of the fallen angel/human women co-mingling produced a hybrid that would have been part angel and part human how did that *work*? I'm not talking about how the angels managed to impregnate human women (some things are better left unknown). I'm talking about the creature that would have been *produced* by such a union. What *was* it? Was it angelic, or human? I believe it was *both*. It would have obviously had a human-type body, though probably different from ours. It would have also had a *spirit, or soul*.

Since the Nephilim's father was a fallen angel, there would have been no way that it would have possibly come under the umbrella of God's *redemption*, even though the Nephilim also had a spirit or soul. While Christ died for *humanity*, there is nothing in Scripture to indicate that the results of His atoning death also extend to fallen angels. In fact, Paul even alludes to "*elect angels*," (cf. 1 Timothy 5:21), which gives us the impression that *some* angels were chosen by God *without the ability* to ever fall.

I believe that it is as simple as this: God purposefully created the majority (or two-thirds) of angels perfect in holiness throughout all time and eternity. They *will* never, nor *would* ever consider, sinning against God. They do not *possess* that capacity, much like believers will no longer possess that capacity in the next life.

While all are free to disagree, I do not believe they have the capacity to sin, based on this comment from Paul to Timothy. At the same time, I believe that certain angels were created who were *not* elected to perfection in holiness. Either these were created *to* fall, or they were created with a *free will*, which would give them the *choice* to choose either for or against God.

I also believe that *any* being having a free will *always* chooses *against* God *eventually*. It is part of the *problem* with possessing a free will. While having or possessing the ability to make free choices is not in and of itself *sin*, the result of some of the choices made by the being who has free will, can and will eventually *result* in deciding *to* sin.

Judging from God's Word, I do not see how it can be any other way. I believe that this is why Paul states in Romans 5:12, "*Wherefore, as by one man sin entered into the world, and death by sin; and so death passed upon all men, for that all have sinned.*" Of course, I realize there is disagreement over what Paul means here. Does he mean to say that God could have placed every one of us in Adam and Eve's place and each of us would have done the exact same thing, or is Paul saying that *because* Adam sinned, the corruption of sin passed along to every human being after them? Does it matter? The result is the *same*. All have sinned, whether we committed sin by *choosing* to sin as Adam did, or because we were all born *with* a sin nature. Frankly, I believe *because* God is all knowing, He knows whether I would have committed the same error as Adam did in the garden, without having to put me there and *watch* me do it. Unfortunately, I believe I would have done the same thing as Adam. In that sense, God is perfectly

The Watchers, Women and Nephilim

Sons of God, or the Angelic beings called Watchers in the Book of Enoch, lust after daughters of men	Daughters of Eve, or human women, are taken by force and and made to interbreed	The result is offspring that is the stuff of myths. They are powerful, tall, intelligent and also fallen and known as mighty men

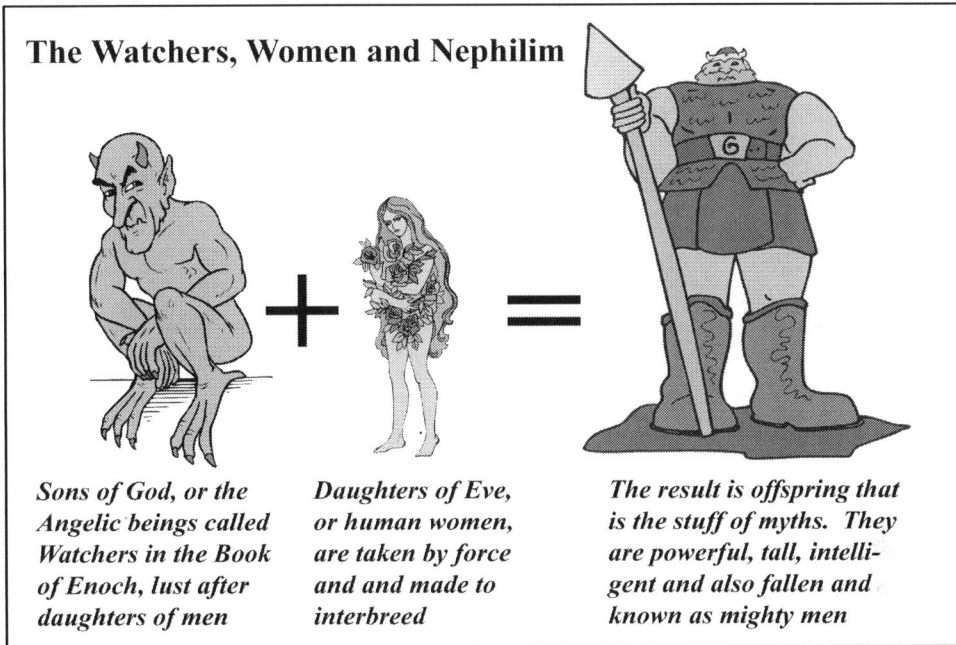

holy and *just* in allowing the sin nature to pass to me, because I would have done the same thing to deserve it.

Conversely, *because* our first parents developed a sin nature, following their decision to believe the Tempter, calling God a *liar*, there is absolutely no way that their sin nature would *not* have been passed down to every other human being that came after them. It would have been automatic.

Double Dose of Corruption

The Nephilim, being born of angelic and human DNA, would have really had a double dose of problems. They would have been born with a corrupt human spirit, affected by the sin nature, *and* they would have inherited the fallen nature of their fallen angelic father. Whether they would have inherited the human sin nature from the mother is really beside the point (depending upon how the sin nature is passed along). They had enough problems by inheriting the corruption from their fallen angel fathers at *inception* and nothing would have changed that. Unfortunately, this situation makes them completely *unredeemable*.

So one of the problems then is if both Peter and Jude are referring to these fallen angels – *the Watchers* – they cannot be the same individuals who are the *demons* the NT and of today. It simply would not work *if* these Watchers have been chained in darkness since that time, when they left their first estate by sinning with human women. Their first estate in this case I believe refers to their position as *angels*. God always creates after its kind. Angels were created as angels, yet these Watchers *chose* to act as if they were *human*.

Working our way through the Old Testament, we do not see a good deal of demonic activity. However, if we consider Saul, the first king of Israel, we gain some insight into any demonic activity that may have existed during that time.

We remember from 1 Samuel 10, that Samuel anointed Saul as the first king of God's chosen people. They had complained because they did not have a human king to lead them into battle and apparently, God was not good enough for them. This is often the case with us as well. Irrespective of what God does for us, we *always* fail Him. We always look to greener pastures and we simply fall in sin. This is what the Israelites did, and in spite of God knowing what was best for them, He told Samuel to give the people everything they wanted.

There came a day when the Israelites would have to deal with the Philistines because they neglected to do this when they first entered the Promised Land under Joshua. They neglected to take care of them then, and now the problem had come to the fore. In spite of the fact that due to Israel's sin in not taking care of the Philistines, God used this situation to bring His man David to the forefront of the situation.

Goliath: Putting It Into Perspective

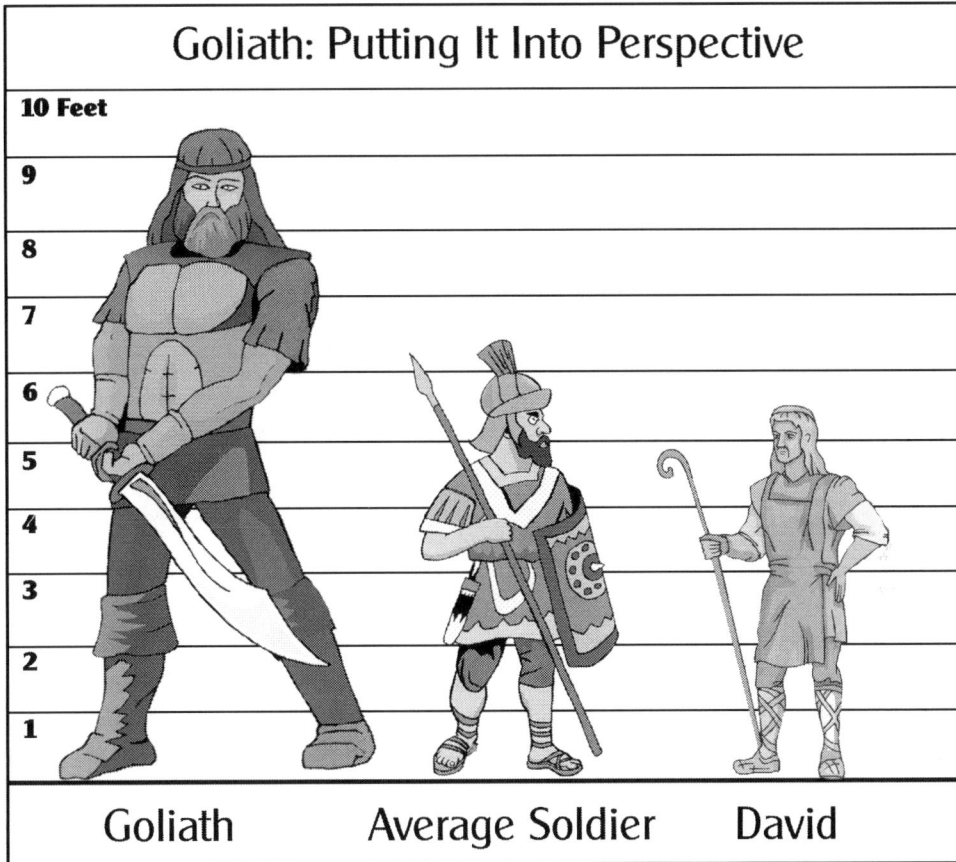

10 Feet
9
8
7
6
5
4
3
2
1

Goliath   Average Soldier   David

In 1 Samuel 17, we read of the very short fight between David and Goliath and what led up to it. Saul, who *should* have gone out to fight the Philistine Goliath, sat in his tent on one side of the Valley of Elah, while the Philistines camped on the other side. It was a stalemate.

Goliath decided to have some fun with the situation, since it was obvious to him that so far, the Israelites *and* their king had shown that *yellow* was their favorite color. He thought it would be a great way to entertain his fellow troops while they waited for Israel's human king to do something, *anything*.

Goliath, of whom the Bible states was "*a champion out of the camp of the Philistines, named Goliath, of Gath, whose height was six cubits and a span,*" (1 Samuel 17:4). Six cubits and a span are just less than ten feet tall. If we consider the fact that, the tallest basketball players currently in the NBA as I write this are Yao Ming and Shawn Bradley, both 7' 6" tall. For most of us, that is *very* tall. Yet, Goliath is said to be two feet *taller* than these two basketball players.

More Giants

Manute Bol, who played for ten years in the NBA, was 7' 7" tall, yet when looking at him, he looks like the proverbial pencil, he is so thin. Robert Wadlow was the tallest human being that we have on record at 8' 11.5" tall. He was then merely six or seven inches *shorter* than Goliath was. Wadlow's body also seemed to be in perspective compared to his height, weighing in at 490 pounds. Yet he still looked a bit *lanky* for his height.

I don't believe Goliath looked out of scale or proportion. In fact, the Bible states that he was a *champion*. That says something. He was a champion fighter, trained from his youth. If you wanted to be safe during a battle, probably hanging out near Goliath (or one of his four brothers) might have been the way to go, or not depending upon how they fought.

Nonetheless, the Scripture says, "*And he had an helmet of brass upon his head, and he was armed with a coat of mail; and the weight of the coat was five thousand shekels of brass. And he had greaves of brass upon his legs, and a target of brass between his shoulders. And the staff of his spear was like a weaver's beam; and his spear's head weighed six hundred shekels of iron: and one bearing a shield went before him,*" (1 Samuel 17:5-7).

Goliath Was No Weakling

Taking in all of the above information tells us that Goliath was no *weakling*! The armor on his chest weighed in at approximately 125 pounds. The weight of the spearhead was about 15 pounds. For those two items *alone*, the weight totals 140 pounds and this does not include the other items he carried. Because he was a champion, he was certainly used to carrying that much weight into battle, and was able to wield it without difficulty.

There Goliath stood, shouting out epithets and taunts to Israel and her human king. He defiantly dared anyone to come out and fight him. No one did.

David arrives on the scene, on an errand from his father and the first thing he notices is that not one soldier in Israel's army had the guts to go out against Goliath. They valued their lives over God's *honor* and *reputation*.

Genesis 6

GIANTS

Master Builders of Prehistoric and Ancient Civilizations

By Stephen Quayle

On the cover of Stephen Quayle's book Giants, *we see an average sized man flanked by two giants. If the man in the middle is approximately 6 feet tall, the giants are at least 8 feet tall.*

It is difficult to be too hard on them, because frankly, without God directing *me* and giving me a strong sense that I would be victorious against Goliath, it is doubtful that I would have run to volunteer to fight him either.

The problem of course, is that God expects us to *trust* Him, which means stepping out in *faith*. Faith allows us to believe that He *will* accomplish His plans and purposes *through* us, whether we *feel* it or not.

We can see why David was considered by God to be a man after God's own heart. David's immediate concern was for the reputation of Israel and more importantly, the *God* of the same. He was concerned that not one soldier seemed to have the inclination to even *want* to

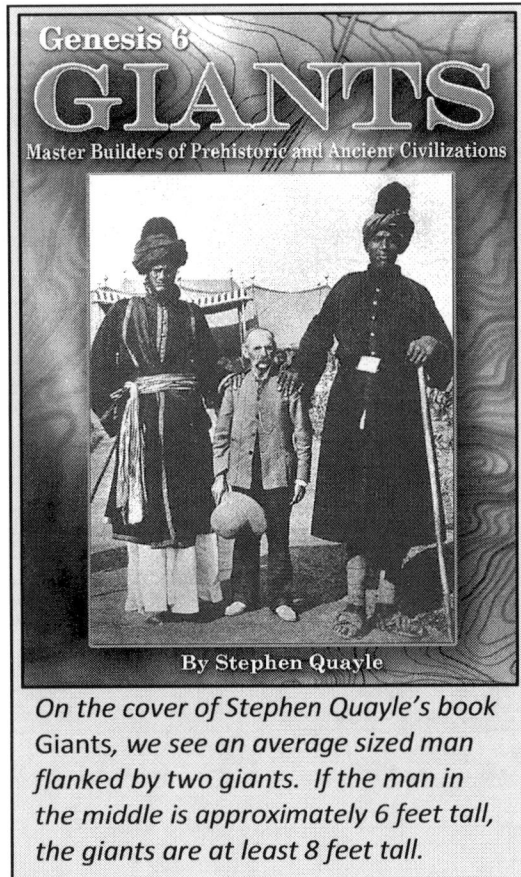

stand up to one of God's enemies. They seemed to prefer instead to cower right behind their king, Saul. This would not do. Someone needed to defend Israel and God's honor.

David to the Rescue!

David decided to act and act he did. We know the story. David, eschewing the suggestion to wear armor, picked up five stones, and went out to slay a giant among men. The first stone he threw nailed the "champion" Goliath right in the head and then David wasted no time in running up to him and cutting his head off. He seemed fearless.

This *one* act of bravery ultimately did three things:

1. *Routed the Philistines*
2. *Made him Saul's target*
3. *Made him the next king over Israel*

At first, Saul was glad that the Philistines were no longer a problem. He gratefully took David under his wing so to speak, and sent him to take care of matters that needed attention within Israel. However soon, because of the cheers of the people, he became jealous of David. Saul had already made a number of mistakes, which cost him fellowship with God and eventually the royal throne. Because of these losses, he was not in his right mind.

It was not too long before we come across these words, "*The next day* **an evil spirit** *from God came forcefully upon Saul. He was prophesying in his house, while David was playing the harp, as he usually did. Saul had a spear in his hand 11 and he hurled it, saying to himself, "I'll pin David to the wall." But David eluded him twice,*" (1 Samuel 18:10, emphasis added).

Note that it was *after* Saul became extremely angry because the people held David in higher esteem, *God* sent an evil spirit to Saul. This evil spirit came upon Saul, with *force*. It is interesting that *God* sent this spirit. It is also reminiscent of the book of Job, where God appears to almost entice Satan into wanting to deal with Job. In fact, God brings up Job's name first (cf. Job 1), and Satan grabs onto it, completely. God sets the limits, and Satan does his best to bring Job down in sin.

Here, an evil spirit sets upon Saul. However, what *is* this evil spirit? Is it one of the fallen angels, *or* is it a disembodied spirit of one of the Nephilim?

Noah's Day

Considering the times of Noah, we know that they were *terrible*. The Bible tells us that all men thought of continually was *evil*, (cf. Genesis 6:5). One can only wonder how humanity became so brutally evil, if not for the intrusion of something much more powerful than mere man would have been.

If we agree that fallen angels *did* somehow find a way to impregnate human women, with the hybrid creature called Nephilim as a result, the bodies of these beings would have been destroyed in the global Flood that God sent upon the earth because of all the evil (unlike their fathers, the fallen angels).

This global Flood left *nothing* alive, except Noah, his family, and the animals in the Ark. There was virtually no place on earth that these hybrid creatures or Nephilim could have gone to have been safe from the rising torrential waters. No matter how powerful they might have been, they would *not* have found a way to stay above the water, so they all eventually *drowned*.

We must also keep in mind that during the time when God opened the heavens and the fountains of the deep, we can assume that the tremendous amount of weight of the water had a *major* catastrophic effect on the geology of the time. If you have ever watched documentaries on terrible floods, which have destroyed buildings and cities, along with people, the sight is not pleasant. The prevailing water seeks its own level and allows nothing to stand in the way of its destructive forces. If there is enough weight in the water, it will successfully destroy anything in its path.

Major erosion would also have resulted. The scene would have been one of powerful and complete *destruction*. We are not talking about the way water acts as it fills an empty bathtub, rising slowly and systematically until the bather turns off the water faucet. We are talking about water that *moves,* often swiftly as it cascades over rocks, cliffs, and in or out of caves.

It is common for rivers, which overflow due to torrential rains, or winter snow runoff, to destroy homes and trees along the bank of where the river used to be. This is of course one of the reasons why water is harnessed and used to create electricity. It has unbelievable power and the amount of destruction it caused during the global Flood was absolutely catastrophic! Nothing would have survived in the flesh, nor would the land have necessarily looked the same as *prior* to the Flood.

What About Their Spirits?

Yet even though the *bodies* of these Nephilim would have perished, their souls (or spirits) would *not* have perished. *D*isembodied from their body of flesh, they became part of the heavenly realms. This is not referring to heaven itself of course, but the *realms* Paul speaks of when referring to the "spirits of the air," (cf. Ephesians 6:12).

Missler also believes that *"The Nephilim, the unnatural offspring, are not eligible for resurrection. The bodies of the Nephilim, of course, drowned in the Flood. What happened to their spirits? Could they be the demons of the New Testament?"*[12]

---

[12] Chuck Missler, *Alien Encounters* (Coeur d'Alene: Koinonia House 1997), 213

Missler believes that the demons of the New Testament were/are actually the disembodied spirits of the Nephilim from the Old Testament. While the fallen angels who cohabitated with human women were chained in darkness until their future judgment, their hybrid offspring became disembodied when their bodies were killed in the Flood.

Without a Body, They Search for Another

Considering the fact that these spirits or souls *did at one point* have a body that they lived *within*, it is no wonder that when we come to the New Testament, we see a good deal of demonic possession. These spirits have been roaming for centuries taking over anything they could take over, *animal* or *human*. Imagine how many people have been possessed by the same demons over the centuries. As the person's body died, the demons moved onto someone else.

Why was there so much demonic activity during Christ's day? First, we are not sure that there was *more* activity during Christ's day than at any time before Him, simply because the Bible is silent on it. However if there was, it would likely be due to the fact that God in the *flesh* was now among these demons and His presence created *abject* fear in them.

In Luke 4, we learn that these demons knew who Jesus was without having to be told. They were afraid of Him and they wondered if He was there to torment them *before their time.* In Matthew 8, Jesus casts out demons from the possessed men who lived in a nearby cave and were so ferocious that chains could not keep them subdued. After they implored Him, Jesus allowed these particular demons to go into a herd of pigs, which ultimately ran off a cliff in a crazed mindset, (cf. Matthew 8:21).

It seems clear that demons *possess* people *and* animals because they feel more at home *in* a body than *out* of one. When they are forced to vacate a body, as in Noah's day *through* death, or when they are cast out of a person, they roam around trying to find another home. They may also go back to the same human where they were cast out to see if they can get back in. Jesus points this out to the crowds in gospel of Matthew when He states, "*When the unclean spirit is gone out of a man, he walketh through dry places, seeking rest, and findeth none. Then he saith, I will return into my house from whence I came out; and when he is come, he findeth it empty, swept, and garnished. Then goeth he, and taketh with himself seven other spirits more wicked than himself, and they enter in and dwell there: and the last state of that man is worse than the first. Even so shall it be also unto this wicked generation,*" (Matthew 12:43-45).

The fact that these spirits *want* to live in a body so badly may indicate that they *were at one point* in bodies themselves and they miss the feelings and sensations that only a physical body can provide. It makes sense that they want to experience again what they once had in a body, physical *feelings* and *sensations*.

It is my contention that these demons are the disembodied spirits or souls from the bodies they once possessed as Nephilim. If this is so, there must be a connection between Nephilim and the possibilities of aliens.

I firmly believe that the disembodied spirits of Nephilim (whose original bodies were destroyed in the Flood), have since roamed the atmospheric heavens in order to find other *bodies* to live in. Since they have been *dispossessed* of their original bodies, they must be the demons that Christ, Paul and others came up against in the New Testament. Since they are spirits, they cannot die, so they exist until the judgment. They have also likely been forced to do Satan's bidding as well, since he is the ruler or prince of the power of the air.

Chapter 4
Why the Masquerade?

As indicated, I am operating under the belief that these beings that show themselves to be aliens from other galaxies and/or planetary systems, are nothing more than the *Nephilim* of old. I believe that their original bodies were destroyed in the global Flood and because of that, they seek to gain entrance into other human bodies as their first choice, though other bodies will work too.

However, this does not explain *why* they are or could be presenting themselves as *aliens* who supposedly come in peace. In fact, it does not make sense at all, unless we understand *why* they are going through with this process of deceiving humanity.

If we consider the spirits of the Nephilim as never having been destroyed, then it makes sense that they are obviously *still* among us. Unlike human beings, whose bodies die, with the spirit going to hell or heaven, these Nephilim spirits have *not* yet been placed in hell. Only their "fathers" have been placed in chains and in darkness because of the heinousness of their sin. If these deceased Nephilim are still among us in spirit form, then we might come to the conclusion that all they really want to do is take over someone's body so that they feel at home again, just like they used to when their original bodies were alive prior to the Noahic Flood.

It is easy to think that this sums up the entire issue. However, I believe that the issue is far more involved than this and of course, I am not the first one to have that opinion. If the aliens who visit us *are* Nephilim and even some of the fallen angels who rebelled with Satan (and I believe they are), then we *must* ascertain the reason for their deception, because deception is what they are *creating*. They are attempting to present themselves as something they are *not*, in order to slip something in under the rug so to speak.

Aliens: Deceivers or Truth Tellers?
The alien deception appears to be extremely involved and complex. We have sightings of many different types of space ships, a number of allegedly highly evolved beings of different alien races, and they have purportedly been involved in harvesting DNA and/or genetic material from both men and women for purposes that appear to be creating hybrid beings. Is it possible that history is repeating itself?

If they are *not* aliens and are in fact, *Nephilim*, then we must determine their reason for doing what they are doing. Even if they *are* truly space aliens, we must *still* learn the reason for what they are doing as well. However, as I have said, I am of the opinion that these beings are *not* space aliens at all, but merely disembodied spirits from the original Nephilim (mighty men of old) along with some of the angels who initially followed Satan in rebellion.

I'm sure that like you, over the years I have studied this phenomenon, I have come to a number of conclusions. The conclusions have confirmed for me the *reliability* of Scripture, the *purposes* of God and the *coming* Tribulation and apocalyptic aftermath when Jesus physically returns to earth to establish His kingdom, destroying Antichrist as He arrives to this planet.

From Before the 1950s

In the book *Alien Agenda* by Jim Marrs, he indicates that the Roswell incident was true, and completely hidden by our government. He refers to the MJ-12 and the Aquarius Project, along with numerous individuals involved in it.

He quotes individuals who state without equivocation that in 1947, there was a crash, and the military recovered aircraft of some type, along with four alien-type bodies. These are specifically referred to as non-homo-sapiens in documentation.

Apparently, in 1949, there was another crash (you have to wonder who is flying these things!), which was partially recovered by the military. According to Marrs, one alien survived the crash and supposedly spoke, calling itself EBE. *"This being came from the planet Zeta Reticula star system, approximately 40 light years from Earth. EBE lived until June 18, 1052, when he died [due] to an unexplained illness. During the time period that EBE was alive, he provided valuable information regarding space technology, origins of the Universe, and exobiological matters."*[13]

Marrs also states that in 1958, an abandoned UFO was located in Utah, which still functioned. Though scientists gained some information from it, much was completely unintelligible to them.

---

[13] Jim Marrs, *Alien Agenda* (Harper Collins: 1997), 112

In 1996, alien contact was allegedly established by the United States and our government apparently concluded that these space beings posed no threat to our planet. They kept it secret from the public.

Unfortunately, this information has been debated and argued over as to its authenticity since it became known. There are too many unanswered questions and anomalies to take all of this information seriously. At the same time though, it is not unthinkable that our government would go to great lengths to hide any of this information from the public if it was true.

Let's say it *was* true for a moment. Let's say that an alien was discovered who survived a crash and was taken as part of a military top secret project. Let's also say that the alien *did* provide some information verbally to our government. From reading through Marrs' book, it seems clear that the information this alien provided is not a whole lot different from the information provided to Barbara Marciniak in her book, *Bringers of the Dawn* (discussed later in this book).

Real Alien Bodies and a UFO? That *Proves* Aliens Exist!

So *if* this and other aliens who crashed and either died or survived *were* discovered, what does that mean? Does it mean that these entities are actually aliens? Not to me it doesn't. It could easily mean that the Nephilim demons either found a body to exist in and at the crash, the physical body died leaving the demons expelled to look for other bodies to live within. It could also mean that the existing alien survivor (if this incident is true), was also a demon and when the body died, it was released from that body to search for another.

In other words, it could very well be that the entire Roswell incident and others like it *did* happen, with *Nephilim demons* masquerading as aliens. Convinced that they had found aliens *and* real UFO wreckage, our military hushed it up from the public.

What about the wreckage that was located? Where did it come from? If fallen angels, Nephilim demons, and especially Satan himself can create or at least *manipulate* the physical things in our world, how difficult would it be for them to manipulate the natural resources or materials of our planet *into* something that appeared to be a UFO? Could they then imbue it with additional properties and/or power that it did not originally possess? I for one believe it to be very *possible*.

Marrs' book continues with other aspects and alleged eyewitness testimony from people who state they *saw* the aliens, *handled* the wreckage, and even took pictures of them. Will we *ever* know what is true here? Not if the government can help it.

Even before the early 50s, and only a few short years *after* the Roswell incident, people throughout the country began to experience abductions. They believe they had *literally* been taken from their bed, or from a field they were working in, or some other place entirely, brought up to a space ship and physically probed and examined. Many of their claims appear to be outrageous, yet the more they are considered, the more we realize that there are too many similarities between their experience and others as well.

L. A. Marzulli has a book titled, *The Alien Interview*, in which he interviews many individuals. Some are on the *researcher* side of the situation, while others are on the *experience* side of it. In truth, Marzulli shares some extremely interesting tales with us in his book.

"Mind if I Probe?"
We read of individuals who were abducted from their fields as they farmed and taken up to a waiting space ship. There, they were probed, prodded, and systematically and physically *explored*. Normally, at one point, they engage in some type of sexual activity with female-looking aliens, if the abducted individual is male, or some of their eggs are harvested, if the abducted is female.

Why Did the Original Nephilim Come About?

It would *appear* that the only plausible reason for aliens *wanting* to cohabitate with humans would be to create their own hybrid race, which of course smacks of Noah's time. If this is true, then one has to wonder *why they need to do this*. Why take the time to create a race of mixed human with "alien"? It seems a waste of time and energy, especially considering the fact that the Nephilim demons are *already* a hybrid mix.

This becomes especially questionable if at least part of the main reason that the original fallen angels co-habitated with human women was part of Satan's plan to keep the Messiah from being born into the human family. If *all* human DNA became corrupted, Messiah's birth could not have occurred. How did Satan know about a coming Messiah? From Genesis 3, of course! This proves that whatever God reveals to humanity, He also reveals to Satan. Upon hearing this upcoming judgment, Satan may have put things in motion to preclude the possibility of Messiah being born.

Is it impossible to think that Satan might have spent time *tempting* the Watchers? After all, didn't he also convince 1/3 of the angels to revolt with him? It seems natural, that he would try to tempt these Watchers to go beyond their duties. To the Watchers, they gave into their lust, and maybe had no clue as to Satan's intent that they should intermingle with human women to create a hybrid race.

All Satan would have to get them to see was that these women were extremely good looking and because they were angels, they had the power to take whichever women they wanted. What could a human man do to stop them? Absolutely nothing. As far as the Watchers were concerned, they succumbed to their own lust. As far as Satan was concerned, they served his purposes in infecting the human DNA that God had created a certain way. It was now on its way to being fully corrupted throughout "all generations." Noah though, was considered perfect in his generations, so it appears as though the infection of this corruption had not spread to him.

If we bear all of this in mind, and if that *was* the real reason for the fallen angels co-habitating with women (to stop the Messiah from being born), there is actually no need at all for fallen angels or Nephilim demons or Satan to *need to* or even necessarily *want* to infect the human race again. Messiah has already been born! He was born, lived a sinless life, was falsely accused, died on Calvary's cross, shedding His blood for the remission of sins, was buried and rose again on the third day! Nothing can hinder his return, not one thing!

Possessing and Oppressing

Beyond this, demons are already very capable of *possessing* and *oppressing* people. Many of these people under the control of resident demons have tremendous strength and agility. I have seen only a few people in my life that I believed to be possessed.

There are videos on the Internet, in which people are allegedly possessed and the sounds that come out of their mouths are literally otherworldly. It is difficult to know what is true and what is false, when dealing with the Internet, and if not for the fact that I have witnessed people under the influence of demonic possession, I would have a difficult time believing *anything* from the Internet.

If demons are capable of possessing and controlling people, and endowing them with abilities they had not previously had, then one can only wonder why aliens (if that is what they are), actually need to go through the process of creating hybrid creatures as was done during the days of Noah? As mentioned, the Messiah has been here already. Creating a hybrid race is not going to change that and it will actually make a *weaker* form of who they are now. Though they would likely be more powerful than humans would, they would be *less* powerful than their supernatural parent.

During Noah's time, the Nephilim resulted from the fallen angel-human women union. However, the Nephilim are here *now* and have been since the days of Noah. Why would they need to create something that is a hybrid to introduce into our society, so that they could supposedly *quietly* take it over our planet from within society? Does this make sense to anyone else?

Many are under the impression that the reason these entities are here, in spite of what they tell us has more to do with their desire to take over the planet. They will do this to infiltrate our society with hybrids, and then take over the earth. However, as stated, this entire cloaking, or masquerade makes little sense. What is the point to taking the time to allegedly create a hybrid race of individuals who are stronger and more capable than human beings are now, yet not as strong as the *source* of their inception?

Is It All A Smokescreen?

In other words, from all the individual experiences, I have read of and researched, it appears that *none* of these aliens has any trouble at all *breathing* our air, or moving around our planet with *ease*. Their very presence boasts of technology we can only dream of having and that technology *seems* to work and work *well* (when they aren't crashing, but that's likely operator error, right?).

Why would aliens *need* to go to the trouble of taking *genetic* material *from* human beings in order to create a hybrid race, if this is actually, what they are doing? Could *all of it* – every single ingredient of it – be part of a massive *deception*? Could they be attempting to make us *think* that they are harvesting human female eggs, or other genetic material, but in *truth,* they are doing no such thing? Maybe they are only making it *appear* as though this is what they are doing.

Researchers such as Dr. David Jacobs and Jacques Vallee believe that these aliens intend to take over our world. They believe they will accomplish this by creating hybrids that *look* and *act* like human beings. These will then blend into society because they will so closely appear as if they are human beings. As more and more of them continue to blend into society, they will have the power in necessary numbers to succeed in the overthrow of all society throughout the world. This might seem reasonable at first glance (mainly because we are so familiar with that scenario from movies, comic books, graphic novels and TV shows), but is this what is *really* going on? I do not believe it to be the case.

Men in Black

Some believe that it is a foregone conclusion that aliens have begun infiltrating the societies of the world. It is very much like a *Men in Black* scenario. To the average citizen, these aliens are invisible because they blend in so well. Only those who are part of the *Men in Black* organization in those movies really know what is going on throughout the world.

In our world, there are many who believe that these aliens slip up

sometimes and we gain a glimpse of their *actual* identity. Go to any number of online video hosting companies and do a search using words like *reptilian, aliens among us*, or something similar. The results may include videos in which people believe that the individuals in the video *change,* or *morph.* People attempt to point out a *forked* tongue, or double or even triple *eyelids.* Numerous videos show dark splotches developing on a person's face as the video was originally recorded.

Whether these incidents allegedly captured on video are *real, doctored,* or merely *imagined* is difficult to assess. The quality of the videos is normally *poor*, and because of that, it is difficult to know what is actually occurring. That aside, there are many who believe that what they see in many of these videos is *actual.* Whatever the case may be, if at least some of them are real, they still do *not* prove that aliens want to take over the earth, or that they are infiltrating society to do so. That still brings us back to the *same* questions asked above. Why would aliens *need* to infiltrate human society in order to take it over? It actually seems to be counter-intuitive. If they are not going to take us over, then why are they infiltrating (if they are)?

Again, why would they need to go through all this trouble? *Do* they actually possess the technology they *appear* to have, which allows them to travel from one galaxy to another in ships that *never* seem to run out of fuel? Does that technology allow them to move in any direction *instantly* without having to make huge turning arcs (and often with no noise, and no visible shadow on the ground below)? If true, then this tells us a great deal about their abilities. It could also be telling us a great deal about their ability to *deceive* on a very grand scale. In fact, it is a *global* scale. What if when all is said and done, all of this is nothing more than simply a smokescreen?

Some researchers are of the opinion that these aliens mean us no *good.* Their intent is evil, malevolent, and anything *but* altruistic. They believe they are involved in a huge, very complex scheme to overthrow the powers of the earth, and they will do it by infiltrating society, taking it over from *within*. Does this sound *plausible* to you?

What, Aren't They Already Powerful Enough?

Does it sound as if allegedly super-intelligent beings from other worlds or galaxies *need* to go through the time and trouble of creating hybrid beings in order to move about seamlessly in our world until such a time is right when they can spring their trap on us, so to speak?

Beings with this amount of allegedly superior intelligence and technology do *not* need to masquerade as anything in order to harvest DNA, or genetic material from humans for the purpose of creating a hybrid race that will allow them to move within our society unnoticed. They simply do not need to do that at all, when they could simply *divide and conquer* us now.

The technology that appears to exist, according to both Jacques Vallee and L. A. Marzulli (based on their research), allows the alien UFOs to *appear*, *disappear*, and *reappear* at will. Some are reported to be extremely large, while others are very small.

In numerous instances, both Vallee and Marzulli report a complete absence of shadows by overhead space vehicles, yet they are in the path of sunlight.

Other interviews and research yield additional information about some of these space ships. Almost without fail, abductees report being taken aboard ships where the lighting is *perfect* and *uniform*. When does *that* happen? In fact, many detailed descriptions seem almost *too* perfect to be real. I think it is because they are not actual physical manifestations, but extremely realistic illusions.

In another instance, a couple driving down the highway seemed to be the only ones who saw a UFO flying nearby, next to and then over the highway they were traveling. This interview of Matt & Laura from

Marzulli's book highlights their testimony that a triangular-shaped UFO buzzed their car as they drove down Interstate 5, in California. Originally believing it to be a crop dusting plane, they soon realized that it was a UFO, as it did flips and intricate flying maneuvers over and around their car, coming to stops in mid-air.

At one point, they state, "*We were the only people who saw it! No one else was stopping to see it. We were screaming...we were amazed. I felt like we had to get out of there. I was scared but excited at the same time. It was like being in a fire. The object, the UFO, had a weird presence around it. I really can't describe it, but it was weird. I felt like were targeted...maybe because we're Christians.*"[14]

There are two things that standout in the above account. First, Matt and Laura indicate that no one else in any of the other cars around them seemed to notice the UFO. If they *did* see the UFO, they appeared not to act as if they did, which makes no sense (unless of course, the people in the other cars were all hybrids and knew what was going on!). Secondly, these people believe that they were *targeted* due to their Christianity.

Beings with this much power, through either extremely high intelligence, or technology or both, could simply come in and *take over* the planet before we would be able to scramble our first jets into the sky. If this is so (and I realize it is an "if"), it means that they have *ulterior* motives *and* identities, which are masked with a good deal of subterfuge.

It just seems reasonable to assume that it is more than possible that these entities have gone to the trouble of creating this massively complex, global *hallucination* in which they *want* the world to believe *the same thing*. They want the world to believe they are aliens, and I do not even think it matters if the world believes them to be

---

[14] L. A. Marzulli, *The Alien Interviews* (Spiral of Life, 2009)

malevolent or good. It serves their purpose if humanity simply believes that aliens *exist* and they are *here*.

Behind their alien mask stands, the real reason they have gone to all this trouble and it has *nothing* to do with their alleged concern for us, or their willingness to help. In fact, it has nothing to do with their pretense as aliens either.

The fact that they have not genuinely made their presence known worldwide casts major doubt on their *motives*. There is actually no good reason that these beings would need to hide behind anything at all, if their *ultimate* intent was to take over this world (or to help us, for that matter). They could simply march in (or fly in) and *do it*! Who would actually be able to stop them, if even *half* of what we have heard or read about them and their abilities are true?

Why, Why, Why?
All of these questions keep coming back to the one *main* question, which is *why*. What is their *purpose*? *Why* are they doing *what* they are doing, the *way* in which they are doing it? It is extremely difficult to believe (as I used to believe when I was a kid), that these beings are simply intelligent *aliens* from other planets. It makes infinitely more sense to understand these beings to be *Nephilim demons* and fallen angels, who have returned in preparation for Satan's last showdown with God.

Let's face it, Satan and all the fallen angels have a great deal to lose if their mission fails. If they win, then they get whatever they want. We know from Scripture that they will *not* win, but we also know from Scripture that they will *attempt* to win by overthrowing Christ at His return. It is because they *must* win, that they are doing what they are doing now. The tremendous amount of deception that has gone into this alien connection is astounding. Yet, it has and is working for much of the population of this planet. Had they simply swooped in as they are – fallen angels and demons – no one would have bought any of it. This way, as benevolent aliens, they can whitewash their actual motives with reasons that sound compassionate, intelligent, loving and all the rest. Who would *not* accept that?

At the same time, they cause Christians to think that the Nephilim are at it again, in their attempts to rebuild another hybrid race that will infiltrate society in order to be able to pounce on humanity at just the right time. I may be completely wrong, but I just do not buy it. I believe they are toying with all of us. All of these alien/ascended masters, including talk of another hybrid race is presented to allow them to bide their time.

Certainly, what these entities want is for a world of people to be ready to *receive* the Antichrist. That is what they are working to accomplish. They have determined that the best way to bring that about is to create this complex maze of alien phenomenon. Society has become so used to the alien concept. Needing to actually create a hybrid race – another Nephilim, if you will – is not necessary, in my view. As stated, I may be completely wrong and I am certainly willing to acknowledge that possibility.

Someone might well ask why Nephilim would need to hide behind the masquerade they have created. Why do they need to appear to people as benevolent (yet scary), aliens who have come to here to help us? Why do their plans for helping us mean that on one hand they are attempting to *integrate* themselves into our society, while on the other hand, they are attempting to present their very presence in extremely altruistic terms? How could they be *both* altruistic and benevolent, while at the same time, busy creating hybrids, which they will co-mingle with our society?

Chapter 5

What Are They Teaching?

R epeatedly, I have read of the experiences individuals have had when they were allegedly abducted and there are several things that are similar across the board. Of course, I'm not the only one who thinks this. These aliens outwardly **seem** to be involved in two primary efforts:

1. *An interbreeding program*
2. *Delivering messages of a religious nature*

These two things summarize the nature of these visitations to the citizens of earth, but do they really? While people like Vallee and Jacobs believe their presence is one that should cause us to *fear* for our physical safety and lives, others believe that there is something far more sinister at hand, which involves the spiritual realm. Still others welcome these beings with open arms, believing that they not only hold the key to the earth's problems, but to the *inner* problems of the soul as well.

It's All About the Spiritual

If these beings *are* Nephilim – demons who are masquerading as space aliens – then it makes sense that their focus would be on the *spiritual* and *religious* aspect of our lives. I have yet to read of any alien sharing knowledge of their futuristic technology, or their ability to cure the common cold. While we wait for that information to be shared with us, these bits of illumination never seem to come our way.

What we *do* gain from them is the same gobbledygook that has been part of the New Age movement for decades, yet because it is *spoken* directly by some of these beings, it is fully accepted by most without so much of a "hmmm, I wonder if that's true" mentality.

What is also fascinating is how often these "ascended masters," (or whatever label they apply to themselves), normally *stop* providing counsel to humans just when it starts to get *interesting*. They will give their little talks and speeches, in which they speak of the higher things that we are unable to comprehend now, then mysteriously (yet expectantly) sign off, promising to return another day with more information. They are also *masters* of repetition. They seem to be experts at saying the same thing numerous ways. The book *The Starseed Transmissions – An Extraterrestrial Report*, lists chapter after chapter of transmissions or channeled messages from a being named Rafael.

Rafael Speaks

In this book, this particular *being* (named Rafael), that transmits messages to the human author of the book, takes a different route than do the Pleiadians from Marciniak's book. Regarding Christ, Rafael states, *"Christ is the single unified being whose consciousness all share. He is the being who sacrificed, for a time, his unified sense of identity, and cloaked himself in the matter of a planet that a species might share his life. He went to sleep to dream an evolutionary process that would leave him, upon awakening, clothed in a physical body comprised of many human cells.*

"Christ's first coming was the first time since life appeared on Earth that the totality of consciousness woke up in the frame of a man. This was Jesus of Nazareth.

"Through Jesus, Christ walked the Earth and began to prepare the human population. He taught the matterbound humans of the Roman Empire to do the opposite of all their habitual inclinations; love your enemy, give away all your material possessions, be humble, and so forth. He taught people how to break every single one of the governing principles which Satan was at that time using to regulate the known world."[15]

The above information is barely scratching the surface of the full contents of *Starseed Transmissions*. You will note a number of things about the way in which this Rafael has explained Jesus and His mission on earth. First, note that Jesus is a *unified* or *collective* consciousness. Note also the implication that Jesus is really the *least* of all the "masters" ("the first time since life appears on Earth"). When you get to the portion of this book, which deals with Barbara Marciniak's *Bringers of the Dawn*, you will note similarities and differences in the messages of both Rafael, and the Pleiadians. You will note that Rafael's message is far more religious in nature, while

---

[15] Kenneth X. Carey *The Starseed Transmissions* (Uni-Sun/Stillpoint Book, 1982), 66

the Pleiadians refrain from dwelling on religion per se, preferring instead to represent nearly everything from a *humanistic* standpoint, to a world in which there are atheists, agnostics and people of all religious spectrums, as well as those who see the world strictly through New Age eyes. While people who might read both books *may* also notice the dissimilarities between the books, these differences will pose no problem for them to reconcile, because the same concepts exist and are espoused in both.

One thing that stands out in *all* the books that I have read, allegedly channeled by these *"masters"* or aliens. In all cases, the language is perfect English, and stated with a matter-of-fact quality. It is presented as *authoritative*, which give human beings absolutely no reason to doubt the veracity either of the entities sending these messages, or of the messages themselves.

Yes, Master

There are unfortunately, too many gullible people in this world who *because* of their gullibility, have the unqualified audacity to refer to these entities as "master" all because the entities speak through a human channel and *sound* authoritative. Because they verbalize when human beings are sitting in front of them, people opt to believe what they are saying without questioning the contents or the source, because they *want* to believe it.

They believe they are in the presence of some entity that is far superior to them on the spiritual plane. They are *honored* to be in their presence. The reality is that when all is said and done, they are hearing what they *want* to hear, nothing more and nothing less, and they are giving honor to none other than Satan. They put their own meaning to the words they hear and because the messages are normally generic, nearly any meaning could easily be applied to them. Even those messages that are far more specific leave room for people to interpret them the way they want to interpret them. The fact that in Marciniak's case, the Pleiadians emphasize that their messages will always be changing, supports the idea that interpretation is fully subjective, and based on what the hearer needs at that moment.

I have heard many audio recordings and watched videos of these sessions. I have also read many transcripts of these events, where these entities allegedly deign to stoop to humanity, and not *once* has anyone in the listening audience ever stood up and questioned the motives of these beings, or asked for their credentials, that I have heard.

"You Hear and Obey, Got It?"

When these beings speak through a human channel, every word they speak is accepted as pure *truth*, yet the same individuals, who receive every word spoken by these beings with unquestioning *gladness*, will resolutely deny the idea that the Bible could even remotely be *genuine* or *inerrant*. While they may refer to the Bible from time to time, it is for the purpose of picking and choosing what they need for that particular moment. Taking Scripture out of context is the norm.

In essence, while they spend their lives doubting the Bible's authority and veracity, they take the word of an entity verbatim, in spite of the reality that the entity has done *nothing* to prove his own identity, or his own message.

Personally, I believe these beings could read from the *phone book* and people would respond with, "*Oh, yes, master. Thank you!*" It is ridiculous and yet it is to these people we are called to witness, praying that the Lord will put them in the frame of mind that allows them to see the *error*, so that they might embrace Jesus Christ and the salvation that is only available through Him.

Fellow Christian, this is our calling and these deluded people are part of the mission field, wherever we find them and it only by God's grace that we are not deluded with them! We have no idea which of those individuals God will save, so the message must be presented to all of them.

The following message was allegedly transmitted to Benjamin Crème, leader of Share International, in 1979 from the long-awaited "ascended master," known for now as Maitreya:

"'How,' Maitreya asks, 'can you be content with the modes within which you now live: when millions starve and die in squalor; when the rich parade their wealth before the poor; when each man is his neighbor's enemy; when no man trusts his brother? For how long must you live thus, my friends? For how long can you support this degradation?'"[16]

TOM-TOM CRUZ CHANNELS A SPACE ALIEN DURING A SEMINAR

©2010 F. DERUVO

---

[16] http://www.share-international.org/maitreya/Ma_teachings.htm

The previous message of "hope" is reportedly from Maitreya and though not stated to be an *alien*, he *is* stated to be the *final master* for this world. Through him and under the auspices of his eventual world leadership, this planet will evolve into a state of perfection and paradise.

We would expect a figure such as someone claiming to be Maitreya to speak in verbiage that promotes a *social* agenda, in which all humanity can get along by fulfilling one another's needs. Unfortunately, what people will initially see as altruism and thoughtfulness toward others, will eventually be seen for what it is, the vehicle that allows Maitreya to gain total control. This final ruler (if it is Maitreya), will be Antichrist and this world will shake, rattle and roll as never before!

Incidentally, just recently as I write this, Crème announced that Maitreya has *physically* appeared on the planet. He did so quite unobtrusively and with no fanfare, by appearing on an American talk show. There he spoke about his book *The Value of Nothing.* His name is *Raj Patel*. Crème and many of his followers believe this man to be the Maitreya, the one the entire world has been waiting to appear for so long (whether they think so or not). According to Crème, he is finally here, in the form of a man.

Patel has been involved in numerous organizations, which promote food for the starving and other groups that have as their platform some type of social agenda. There is certainly nothing wrong with wanting to feed the hungry, however, Patel's total involvement in these organizations seems to stem solely from a socially motivated one.

This particular announcement was made on January 14, 2010, on the home page of Share International:

"He was introduced not as Maitreya, the World Teacher and Head of our Spiritual Hierarchy, but simply as a man, one of us. In this way He 'ensures that men follow and support Him for the truth and sanity of His ideas rather than for His status'. He spoke earnestly of the need for peace, achievable only through the creation of justice and the sharing of the world's resources. This is the first of many such interviews which will be given in the USA, Japan, Europe and elsewhere, bringing His message of hope to the world."[17]

With this brief introductory message, the next (allegedly) leader of the world emerges from the shadows. Does he actually leave the shadows behind?

The lack of caution of human beings evidence is often astounding. Yet, this is what deception produces, a mindset fully controllable by others. I want to be careful not to *judge individuals*, recognizing that the only reason I am not also swept up in the deception has to do with God Himself. Yet, it is clear that people *want* to go out of their way to believe what these aliens or Maitreya endeavor to teach us. The folks who gobble up every word spoken by one of the "aliens" never take the time to determine whether or not what they are hearing is plausible, or whether it even makes sense! Even if they wanted to do so, how would they be able to do that? Do they determine to find out if one "alien" winds up contradicting what another "alien" states? Yet, where the Bible is concerned, these same people will go over it with a fine-tooth comb in every attempt to negate it, or toss it to the side simply because they find it difficult to believe that something written so long ago could have any possible value for them today.

What is *so* valuable about the message of these particular spiritual entities that people feel the need to sit on the edge of their chairs absorbing every uttered word offered to them? Is what is taught so

---

[17] http://www.share-international.org/index.htm

breathtaking in nature and so spectacular in form that edification is automatic and instantaneous for anyone who listens?

THE Lie

It is as if anyone would be a complete *moron* to ignore what these allegedly advanced beings *espouse.* However, what we *can* understand from this is that the *reason* these individuals appear to be so gullible is due to the fact that God has sent them a delusion that causes them to believe *the lie.* They are powerless to refute what they hear because they have rejected God! They are unable to differentiate between truth and error. For so long they have ignored God, and for so long they have refused His wooing and His desire to embrace them, that they have been caught up in error. They have rejected truth repeatedly and embraced error, and because of their deliberate *rebellion*, God has given them *over* to their error.

However, as Christians, we cannot – we *dare* not – ignore these people. We *must* continue to fight for souls by sharing the Good News of Jesus Christ. As we work to prepare their hearts to receive the seed of God's Word, we must always remember that as long as someone is *alive*, they have a chance to receive the salvation that Christ offers.

The Teachings

We need to realize that these Nephilim are in the business of *deceiving* as many people as they possibly can. The reason for this becomes clear when studying their claims, their admonitions, their teachings, and their warnings.

One of the interviews in L. A. Marzulli's book concerns a woman named Lynne Dickie. She was, at one time, involved in *channeling* messages from aliens, she originally thought were good, and on the up and up. These messages came in the form of thought and visions and because of them, she began to understand what they wanted to achieve *through* her, to society.

I come from the Presence where there is **no time** but the eternal now. I retain, even in the midst of this relationship, an awareness of this realm and of the Universal Being that inhabits it. I come with a message that will prove vital to you in these final days of your history. My individual identity comes into being only as I enter the context of my relationship with you. When I am no longer needed in this capacity, I will merge back into the Being behind all being. There I will remain in...*

What this channeler thinks is an alien, is really a devil or demon. The Nephilim are back with a vengeance, and we need to understand their ultimate goal!

Alleged transmission from extraterrestrial, Rafael, to Kenneth X. Carey in the book "The Starseed Transmissions," page 3, ©1982, Uni-Sun/Stillpoint Publishing (emphasis added)

©2010 F. DERUVO

It seems as though from the first moment they began contact with her, their messages were *religious* in nature. They told her they contacted her because *God* had chosen her. They told her they were angels, and they also informed her that it was part of her job to take pictures of all the UFOs she would see in the sky and share those pictures with the world.

These entities also indicated that there was going to be a major pole shift, which would result in major disasters throughout the earth. What became really interesting was the fact that these aliens began to tell her of three upcoming *evacuations* of people from the earth. Dickie states that these events are referred to as "the Ascension". *"The Ascension of the Christed Ones was what it was called. We would be taken up into the one to three mile wide ships and would be transformed into light bodies, we would be gone for 1,000 years and then we would come back and live side by side with other E.T.s"*[18]

That's interesting, isn't it? They spoke of an event, which was slated to occur three different times. During these removals or evacuations, people would be literally taken up to waiting space ships above the earth, where they would exchange their physical bodies for bodies of *light*.

Dickie further indicates that though she was a Christian from a young age, she had wandered from the path of righteousness. She took up partying and hanging out with people she refers to as hoodlums and essentially turned her back on God.

She states that *"when the Beings started talking to me, they knew they had to conform to my beliefs, because even though I had strayed far from God, I still believed in Him."*[19] This was an important factor because when the beings began communicating with her, they used *religious* verbiage to gain her trust, eventually telling her that God had chosen her for a specific task. The task she was given was to begin photographing space ships and she began doing that in 2005.

Dickie's experience made her realize that *Satan* had ultimately *deceived* her. Though she was not a Satanist, nor did she knowingly worship him, he gained access to her because walked away from God and His righteousness. Did she lose her salvation? If she was an authentic Christian, then the answer is no. What she lost was fellowship with God and His protection. It is obvious that God allowed her to go that route in order to *learn* valuable and eternal lessons. The same thing occurred with the Prodigal Son, who *never* lost his connection with his father and family, though he walked

---

[18] L. A. Marzulli *The Alien Interviews* (Spiral of Life, 2009; Lynne Dickie Interview)
[19] Ibid

away for a time. When he returned, the lessons he had learned kept him from ever walking away again.

Replacing God with the New Age

Dickie replaced God with New Age techniques, including Reiki, a Japanese form of stress reduction. Reiki is also a means by which Satan and/or his angels find a way to enter into a person's sphere of control. Eventually, through a series of events, and the witnessing of a co-worker, she was freed of her demonic connection to UFOs and aliens. Originally believing that these aliens were benevolent beings, she now understands that they were and are *demons*, merely impersonating angels.

All of this then, again, confirms in my mind that these are Nephilim, making their final move on planet earth. They are working under orders of their leader – Satan himself – to achieve a society in which *the lie* that Satan has told from the beginning, will become the norm throughout the world; that all people are already *gods*.

In order to gain the confidence of the world, and the world's leaders, these Nephilim demons have had to work slowly, for centuries, attempting to instill within the minds of humanity that *other* beings exist. These other beings are more intelligent, and very concerned for our welfare. This tremendous concern has caused them to literally stop what they are doing, and concentrate on earth's problems. The Nephilim need to be seen as *altruistic, caring, concerned* and wanting to help. They need to be understood as higher beings whose purpose here is to educate, not conquer; to free, not imprison.

If at any time, their mask slips off, they are in danger of being seen for whom they are, and that could blow their cover. Yet they have spent so much time preparing people that it is likely the realization of their true identity would not create much fear within many, so used to hearing from them are we that it has almost become second nature to many.   Their true identity would merely be explained as something else, and probably be blamed on the individual's inner fears or something similar.

Masquerade, Demon Style

In fact, if we consider it, these supernatural entities seem to have prepared a unique masquerade for just about every group:

- *To those who do not believe in aliens, they are seen as Ascended Masters*
- *To those who believe in aliens, they are seen as intelligent, benevolent aliens*
- *To professing Christians, or those within the Emergent Church, they are seen as angels or higher powers*
- *To atheists, they don't really need to do much at all because for the most part, these people don't necessarily believe in the supernatural, so they will let them continue in that belief*

I cannot get past the fact that whole thing sounds extremely fishy to me. It prompts me to ask a number of questions:

- *Why are these beings so concerned about earth at all?*
- *Why do they seem to be pushing a <u>religious</u> message?*
- *Why are they offering <u>nothing</u> in the way of medical or technological expertise? If they actually have it, wouldn't that be a wonderful way to help us?*

As far as I can tell, these Nephilim are simply promoting themselves as highly intelligent individuals who can help us solve our problems. The quandary though, is that in every case, they seem to be *thwarted*, or held back by something that is keeping them from bringing their own plans to fruition. They never tell us *what* that something is, but they assure us that the time is simply not right for them to reveal themselves. What are they waiting for, and if something is keeping them from revealing themselves, it must be because that something is far *superior* in power to them. Of course, the aliens blame this inability to reveal themselves on humanity. Apparently, it is due to all the doubters and fear-mongers on this planet, that they are ultimately unable to reveal their full presence.

Let's take a few moments to look at some of their channeled messages. In doing so, we may find what we are looking for right there, without having to search further.

The Rapture

Many Christians today look forward to an event known in the Bible as the Rapture. The Rapture, spoken about by Paul and implied through the teachings of Christ, is the event in which all who are part of the invisible Church – both living and deceased – are raised to meet Christ in the air (cf. I Thessalonians 4:13-18). Paul's closing words in this section indicate that this occurs in order to avoid the "wrath to come."

Of course, a growing number of Christians do not at all believe in the Rapture. They look at it as a contrivance by other Christians who are simply afraid to face the trials and persecutions of the coming Tribulation. The problem of course with this reasoning against the PreTrib Rapture position, is that it does not take into account the trials and tribulations that occur *daily* in the life of *all* Christians. Many Christians throughout the world are undergoing severe trials and persecution now, even to the point of death with many already having lost their lives. Others will likely follow down that path of martyrdom. The argument that the Rapture is simply an "escape clause" really has no merit, yet it continues to be believed. In fact, this false reasoning seems to have done nothing but promoted a sense of pride in the individuals who believe that they *will* go through the Tribulation, while the "poor, misguided PreTrib Rapturist" is unwilling to do so. Obviously then, the anti-PreTrib Rapturist comes to believe that *they* are the spiritually mature ones in Christ because they are ready and willing to suffer at the hands of the Antichrist. The truth of a doctrine is not decided on whether or not it seems *plausible*. The truth of it is either confirmed or not in Scripture alone. If I am wrong, and the Rapture is *not* PreTrib, fine. God will bring me through the Tribulation, or if I am to die during it, will be with me (if I am alive when the Tribulation happens, of course). God is able, and He will not give me more than I can bear.

Many Christians have spent a good deal of time discussing and even quarreling over the possibility of the Rapture, leaning on this verse or that to prove or disprove it. At the end of such quarrels, people are usually no closer to changing their viewpoints, because both parties firmly believe that they are correct in *their* belief.

The Bible is the best resource to look to when attempting to discern any doctrine espoused by anyone. The true test should always be what is found in God's Word. However, at the same time, with so many people seeing the same passages teaching two different things, it helps to go *outside* the Bible to see if any verification can be found for such a doctrine as the Rapture. This is where some of the messages from these *aliens* come into play.

It appears that in their desire to allegedly help us, these aliens also come to us with a warning; a warning that if not heeded, would mean the earth's ultimate demise. In some ways of course, this sounds overly dramatic, and very much like an episode of Star Trek®, or Star Wars®, or some other sci-fi program of similar nature. The problem though is that this is *not* a TV program or movie. The situation as understood or seen by many people is seemingly *real* in nature, and that reality looms larger as the global group of abductees grows with the passage of time.

Pardon My Prodding

According to many people who say they have been abducted, ex-amined, poked, prodded, and given messages (telepathically), the un-derlying communication to the citizens of earth is that these aliens are coming to visit us more and more because of their *concern* for our planet's welfare. They are concerned because they do not want us to destroy ourselves. They are concerned because they also want to ensure that we get to the next *evolutionary* level, so that we will become more like them. This is what they *say* as they begin to transmit their messages to us, from their brain to ours. Here then is where it becomes interesting.

In *Alien Encounters,* Chuck Missler clarifies for us. *"One might expect that such a visitation from our 'space parents' would be accompanied by detailed information on how to solve our increasing global difficulties. With their supposed highly advanced technology, surely they would have solved the kinds of political, economic, environmental, and medical problems we now face. And yet, no such message [has been] given. Instead, Rael [a person so-named by the visiting aliens – ed.] was given a religious message – in effect, a Bible study conducted by an ET!"*[20]

What Is There Message?
Here we are on earth, with poverty-stricken nations, disease running rampant, seeming insurmountable economic difficulties, no cure for cancer, AIDS, or the common cold, yet these aliens seem not to have anything to offer about those things. Instead they are intent upon explaining the "real" meaning of the Bible to at least some of the abductees.

Missler continues; *"The primary message that the extraterrestrials wanted Rael to understand was that they created mankind. According to Rael, the extraterrestrials told him that they created humanity in their image by sophisticated genetic engineering techniques."*[21] Rael continues in his book titled *The Message Given to Me by Extraterrestrials,* by explaining and describing the actual story of Creation,

---

[20] Chuck Missler, *Alien Encounters* (Coeur d'Alene: Koinonia House 1997), 136
[21] Ibid, 136

although not the one most of us have read and know found in the first few chapters of Genesis.

If all this is not interesting enough, we find that another one of the main messages being given to earthlings by aliens is one which might cause fear in many, at first glance. If not for the fact that this message has been distilled through several individuals on earth at various times, it would be extremely difficult to believe. Yet, here is a message given by ETs and recorded in The Ashtar Command, Project World Evacuation, 1993: *"Our rescue ships will be able to come in close enough in the twinkling of an eye to set the lifting beams in operation in a moment. And all over the globe where events warrant it, this will be the method of evacuation. Mankind will be lifted, levitated shall we say, by the beams from our smaller ships. These smaller craft will in turn taxi the persons to the larger ships overhead, higher in the atmosphere, where there is ample space and quarters and supplies for millions of people."*[22]

What was that?! Did someone mention an evacuation of "millions of people"? This is obviously very similar to the messages that Lynne Dickie received, mentioned earlier in this book. These series of Ashtar Command messages transmitted to a person named Tuella is on the Internet and can be easily read by going to the URL listed at the end of this chapter. The entire book starts out with this small disclaimer: *"Although these Messages of the coming Earth Changes and Ascension of Planet Earth given by the Ashtar Command in the 1980's through Tuella (Thelma Terrell) have since been long delayed in their outcome, mainly through the strong efforts of the Forces of Darkness to eliminate or postpone the event, the instruction and program contained therein remains largely unchanged and applicable to the now fast approaching times of final cleansing."*[23]

---

[22] http://www.thenewearth.org/ASHTAR1ProjectWorldEvacuation.html - 06/05/2009
[23] Chuck Missler, *Alien Encounters* (Coeur d'Alene: Koinonia House 1997), 187

The Upcoming Evacuation

Notice what is being stated here. Apparently, these messages were originally transmitted in the 1980s. It was thought then (by the "aliens") that they were revealing what was going to come to pass *soon*. It did not, so this disclaimer was placed as an *excuse*. The average individual however, will look at this and say *"See? The forces of darkness (Christians) are working against world peace! We've got to work harder! We must overcome them!"*

According to Missler, the first messages from the Ashtar Command arrived in 1952 to author George Van Tassel. *"We are concerned about [humanity's] deliberate determination to EXTINGUISH HUMANITY AND TURN THIS PLANET INTO A CINDER...Our missions are peaceful, but this condition occurred before in this solar system and the planet Lucifer was torn to bits. We are determined that it shall not happen again."*[24]

What is engrossing here is that if we compare the information of these messages with the biblical picture, we gain a good deal of insight into what these beings *know*. In spite of the fact that many within Christendom do not believe in the doctrine of the Rapture, here is a type of Rapture being postulated by demons masquerading as aliens!

The fact that these "aliens" have already sent messages about a coming evacuation of millions of people from this planet is obviously their attempt to downplay the *Rapture*, or change the meaning and source of the Rapture. The Rapture according to the Bible is the *instantaneous* translation of true Christians, who make up the invisible Church. This will happen in a moment, in the twinkling of an eye. Paul speaks of this event in 1 Thessalonians 4:15-17: *"For this we say unto you by the word of the Lord, that we which are alive and remain unto the coming of the Lord shall not prevent them which*

---

[24] Chuck Missler, *Alien Encounters* (Coeur d'Alene: Koinonia House 1997), 187

are asleep. For the Lord himself shall descend from heaven with a shout, with the voice of the archangel, and with the trump of God: and the dead in Christ shall rise first: Then we which are alive and remain shall be caught up together with them in the clouds, to meet the Lord in the air: and so shall we ever be with the Lord." This is also reflected in Christ's own Olivet Discourse found in Matthew 24:29-31.

Here we see in a message purportedly transmitted by an alien from the Ashtar Command to a human being that these aliens were preparing the earth for a time in which millions of people would vanish instantly from the face of the earth. If that is not the Rapture, then what is it? While anti-PreTrib Rapturists will say that these beings should not be believed, the fact remains that they are openly teaching a doctrine *not* to Christians necessarily, but to those who are not even aware of the biblical doctrine of the Rapture. If the Rapture is *not* going to occur and it is a figment of someone's overworked imagination, then why waste the time teaching people who have *no religious* training about an event that will not occur anyway? It makes no sense, if the Rapture is not really going to occur.

If the Rapture were going to happen at any other point than *before* the start of the Tribulation, there would be no need for these beings to even mention it at all. Once the Tribulation starts, there will be so much death and destruction that people will not even question why all of a sudden millions of people vanish into thin air! The only time they would question this event, is if it occurred *before* the beginning of the Tribulation, when things are relatively quiet and peaceful. Once the Tribulation starts, pestilences, famines, and death of all kinds are simply part of the picture, from start to finish. Who is going to stop and go, *"Hmmm, even though millions of people have already been killed, I noticed that a few million more are gone just like that. Now that is very strange indeed"*? No one will stop and notice it because they will be way too concerned about making sure their own lives are safe! (Shhh, don't tell this to the anti-PreTribber though.)

So We're the Bad Guys?

Thelma Terrell, (or Tuella as she is known in New Age circles), carried on where Van Tassel left off. *"In the 1980s Ashtar clarified the message to Earth through a new channeler named Thelma Terrell...she compiled the channeled messages of Ashtar, who declared that planet Earth would be spared certain annihilation by an extraterrestrial evacuation of millions of people who **threaten the harmony and evolution of Earth** (emphasis added)."*[25]

Ah, so it becomes clearer. First we learn that the aliens have transmitted messages as early as 1952, which tell of a *removal* of millions of people from the earth, all in on *instant*. Then in the 1980s, another person by the name of Tuella, who has apparently *replaced* the deceased Van Tassel, receives clarified information from this same source that the people who are to be removed are those that threaten earth's existence.

What is fascinating of course is that all of this sounds like the biblical *Rapture* to me. It is a fact that Satan *knows* the Bible and he knows it better than any other living human being (besides Christ Himself). During Christ's temptation in the wilderness, Satan referred to Scripture – God's Word – just as he had in the Garden of Eden. He quoted it in the same manner, *slightly* twisting the meaning of it, so that while it *resembled* its original meaning, it now meant something else.

Jesus immediately saw through it, rejecting Satan's temptations with Scripture of His own, and He used it properly. Satan's deceptive ploys were not strong enough to remove Jesus from His appointed path. The reader is encouraged to read this narrative of Jesus' bout

---

[25] http://www.thenewearth.org/ASHTAR1ProjectWorldEvacuation.html - 06/05/2009

with Satan, and His victory over the same (Matthew 4, Mark 1, and Luke 4).

Satan Knows the Rapture Will Occur

Are the powers of darkness, led by Satan himself, fully aware of an event that Paul speaks of in which all true believers (both dead and alive at the time), will be caught up, to be forever with the Lord? It would appear so, but notice that in Satan's version of this event, those who are raptured or evacuated off the planet are the *problem* children. It is these folks who are keeping the rest of the population and the world itself from *evolving* into the next stage of existence.

It is not merely Chuck Missler and Mark Eastman who provide us with information that indicates a Rapture-like event of the true Church will occur in the future. Others like Constance Cumby have also written about the New Age Movement, critiquing the new world order that New Agers long for and look forward to becoming a reality. This new world order may very well include aspects of Neo-Nazism, along with solid components of the New Age Movement, which is sadly already finding its way into many mainline churches and denominations through the Emergent Church.

Referring to this possible future event Christians call the Rapture, one New Age writer states this, "*The people who leave the planet during the time of Earth changes do not fit in here any longer, and they are stopping the harmony of Earth. When the time comes that perhaps 20 million people leave the planet at one time there will be a tremendous shift in consciousness for those who are remaining.*"[26]

On the Share International website, Benjamin Crème is noted as "a messenger of hope." He is called this due to his connection with the spirit world and his ability to channel the "masters," of which have ultimately become known to Crème as the *Hierarchy of the Masters*.

---

[26] Barbara Marciniak, *Bringers of the Dawn* (Rochester: Bear & Co, 1992)

In the late 1950s, after having spent a number of years studying the writings of Blavatsky, Alice Bailey and others, Crème began receiving what he called transmissions from these Masters. The first of these transmissions informed Crème of an eventual appearance of Maitreya, mentioned earlier, or the *Christ*, of whom Crème referred to as "*Head of our planetary Hierarchy.*"

Between the years of 1959 and 1974, the transmissions occurred with some regularity and Crème became deep friends with the one he called simply, *the Master*. This individual taught Crème things about life, reincarnation, the hierarchy, the higher consciousness and everything connected with the New Age Movement, and coming new world order that he had not learned through the writings of Blavatsky and Bailey.

Not long afterward, Crème began having meetings with others of like mind, to introduce them to the world of the New Age Movement and the coming changes that would occur on this planet. A few years after he began these meetings he received another transmission, but instead of it coming from his master, this one apparently came directly from Maitreya himself. Crème relates this event; "*In June 1974 began a series of overshadowing and transmitted messages by Maitreya, inspiring us, and keeping us informed of the progress of his externalisation. We were privileged also to become aware of the gradual creation and perfectionment of his body of manifestation — the Mayavirupa. In the period from March 1976 to September 1977, these communications from Maitreya became very frequent indeed.*"[27]

This was not to be the only message from Maitreya either as we have seen. There have been many more; "*Between September 1977 and*

---

[27] http://www.share-international.org/background/bcreme/bc_main.htm 06/05/2009

June 1982, British author and lecturer Benjamin Crème received a series of 140 Messages from Maitreya, the World Teacher."[28]

Satan's Hands Are Tied Because of God's Sovereignty

In message number 140, transmitted in May of 1982, Maitreya stated this (in part) through Crème: *"It has been My intention to reveal Myself at the earliest possible moment, to brook no delay, and to come before the world as your Friend and Teacher. Much depends on My immediate discovery, for in this way can I help you to save your world. I am here to aid and teach, to show you the path to the future, and to reveal you to each other as Gods."*[29]

One of the questions that must be asked is twofold; what is keeping the future evacuation from occurring and what is stopping Maitreya from making himself known to the world? Can it be the fact that the Holy Spirit is still here working through the invisible Church? That, and the fact that *if* the Rapture is an actual event, these "aliens" do not know when it is going to occur, just as we do not know. God has kept that information extremely close to His chest.

If Crème is correct that the man named Raj Patel *is* this Maitreya, and *if* this individual eventually turns out to be the Antichrist, then it is clear that it will not be too long before he begins his assent to claim world power. This of course will occur under the personal guidance of Satan himself.

Satan is *not* all-knowing, or all-powerful. He cannot be in more than one place at the same time. Apart from all these things, he does not know every detail about the future. In fact, he only knows what he *sees* in the Bible. He can also attempt to discern from the activity of God's elect angels. As I have stated in another book I have written (*His Highest Purpose*), this is one of the largest reasons why God has chosen to *progressively* reveal His will to humanity. The more God

---

[28] http://www.share-international.org/background/bcreme/bc_main.htm 06/05/2009
[29] Ibid

revealed to humanity, the more Satan knew, so God kept many things to Himself, only revealed things as He saw fit to reveal and only what mankind needed to know at *that* moment. Yes, man was in the dark about any number of things, but so was Satan. This is exactly why faith is the necessary ingredient in our walk with Christ.

Satan Reads the Bible

Because Satan only knows what he learns through the revelation of Scripture, along with what he sees God actually *doing* (through His ministering angelic messengers), he does *not* know the day or the hour of many events which are said to be connected to the End Times.

If the Rapture *is* to occur, as I believe the Bible teaches it will, no one knows exactly when that event will occur. The exact day and hour is not listed in Scripture. The closest we get to it is when Jesus speaks of the times *nearing* the Great Tribulation in Matthew 24. He speaks of the fact that His disciples knew when the seasons were changing by looking at the trees. It is by that change that we know one season blends into another. In the same way, Christ gave us clues or signs to look for which would signal the beginning of the end.

As Arnold Fruchtenbaum states in his book, *Footsteps of the Messiah*, as far as the Jewish rabbis of old were concerned, there were simply two ages; this age and the age to come. This is what rabbis throughout the ages commonly understood.

In Matthew 24, when Christ speaks of the *end of the age*, He is referring to the *end of this age*, which is controlled by *man's* rule (but of course, overseen by God). This age *will* end, when Jesus returns physically to set up His kingdom on earth, and from which IIe will also *physically* rule from David's throne in Jerusalem. This is what separates *this* age from the *next*; Christ's return.

The coming return and reign of Jesus Christ will occur. Satan knows it will occur, and there is nothing he can do about it, except play his part in this upcoming drama.

The signs Jesus spoke of in the Olivet Discourse were given to serve as a way to keep track of things and to watch for, *as this age began to wind down.* Much speculation, argumentation, and debate about what Jesus meant has raged and continues to rage on. Within the past few decades, the belief that most prophetic events have already occurred in the past, leaving only a few chapters in the last part of Revelation to occur, has gained momentum and wider acceptance. The modern trend in much of the visible Church, is believing that Christ's return, far from being the physical return that the two "men" in Acts 1 pointed to, was *spiritual* in nature and occurred in A.D. 70 with the destruction of Jerusalem and the Temple.

This belief *seems* to stem from Scripture (if taken allegorically), but in truth, what many Christians today are advocating is a gradual *improvement* in society. Once we wipe out famine, disease and the like, man himself will be much improved. This improvement will by itself, usher in a new form of *spiritual* Christianity; one in which Christ as the absolute head of the Church, will be able to reign from heaven through all creatures on earth. Unfortunately as stated, this is in marked contrast to what the Bible teaches and the literal meaning that stems from that teaching, in my opinion.

However, mark the similarities between what has just been noted above and the teachings of many of these "aliens." They are too similar to be merely coincidence. In fact, when we take a step back, it quickly becomes apparent that these "aliens" are scratching the itching ears of all groups of people, from those outside the visible Church, to those within it.

Spiritual Fulfillment?

In his book *Satan His Motives and Methods*, Lewis Sperry Chafer pointed out then (in 1919), that a belief in a spiritual form of fulfill-ment had already taken place by Christ, had become the norm. This of course was at odds with the orthodox evangelical position that existed then, which looked to the yet future *physical* return of Jesus. Sperry has this to say regarding this modern belief; "*Well may believers study their own motives in service in view of these vastly differing programs; and question whether there is in them a humble willingness to cooperate in the present purpose of God in pre-paring the Bride for the returning King. Or whether, on the other hand, they have carelessly fallen in with the Satanic ideal which rejects the coming kingdom of Christ by an unholy attempt to establish the present kingdom of Satan.*"[30]

So on one hand, we see humanity – including many within the *visible* Church – catering to and embracing the ideas presented by the enemy that if we all work hard enough, we would one day attain that which we long for in Christ. It is unfortunate that these people are blinded to the truth of the Bible, with its plain, clear message of future events. Then again, the Bible has to first be *read* before it can be understood. Many people simply do not open the Bible in the first place.

Those of us who recognize the message of His Word plainly, under-standing its *meaning* in *literal* terms, look for the signs that Christ spoke of in His Olivet Discourse. While these signs do not necessarily pinpoint the *exact* timing of future events, they let us know whether or not the beginning of birth pains has already begun, or is yet future. We see these signs as simply that; *indicators* allowing us to see the progression of things to their predetermined culmination.

Satan does the same thing. Through his demonic hordes, he keeps abreast of what is going on *throughout* the world and attempts to judge the times and seasons, interpreting what he sees against his

---

[30] Sperry Chafer, *Satan His Motives and Methods* (Grand Rapids: Kregal 1990), 67-68

own understanding of the Bible. Of course, that is the best he can do. He does not know *when* the Rapture will occur and for that matter does not know when many other events will occur, which are related to the End Times. This is why he constantly has to "correct" or "clarify" things as time moves onward, through his *messengers*, leaving unfulfilled the things he transmitted years before, to unknowing and deceived human beings.

New Agers Know What Many Christians Deny

What we know, is that those within the New Age Movement believe that one day, due to "ignorance" and "an inability to evolve," millions of people will be suddenly and instantly *removed* from the face of this planet. Satan has prepared for this upcoming event, by announcing it ahead of time to his followers, though of course, has simply put a completely different *spin* on it.

If the event simply occurred, with absolutely no forewarning or notice given to humanity, it is very likely that a total breakdown in society would occur. As it is, there will be many catastrophic events taking place following the Rapture.

For many of those who have been attending churches part of, or all of their lives, yet did not have an authentic relationship with Jesus, who would have provided authentic salvation, some of these individuals will remember hearing about the Rapture from the Bible. They *will* panic realizing that the Bible prophecy concerning the Rapture had actually occurred! They were in fact, *left behind*. Tim LaHaye and others have it correct, in my view.

It is obvious that Satan has spent decades creating a false understanding of this yet future event. To have his own followers out of the loop so to speak, would not work for Satan's plan at all. He would have to do something to draw attention away from the fact that this concept is taught in Scripture. Because of this, it seems obvious enough that he has done a number of things:

1. *For Christians (professing and true):* Create doubt within them, so that they themselves do not believe the Rapture will occur. Have them focus on the rumor that Margaret MacDonald actually created the concept. Use people to teach them that the doctrine of the Rapture is of dubious origin, and those who believe must themselves be deluded and deceived. If there are Christians who literally deny that the Rapture is going to occur, then this is what they will teach to *everyone.* Confusion, name-calling, quarrels and anger will result.

2. *For the Non-Christians (New Agers):* Get the word out *way* ahead of time the Rapture *will* occur, however underscore the fact that the Bible has it *wrong.* The Rapture will take place to remove Christians from the world, but as far as the world will understand it, these Christians are seen as troublemakers; those who are keeping the planet and people from evolving to the next level. No worries.

Satan's Version of the Rapture

Certainly, this is one reason why Satan began to disseminate his own version of the event of the Rapture. He *knows* without doubt that it *will* take place (unlike many within Christendom, who deny a good deal of the, yet unfulfilled, prophetic discourse). Some Christians to be sure, are not in rebellion to God, nor do they desire to work against Him, but they are blind to His purposes related to the End Times. It is because of this they do wind up *inadvertently* working against Him and His purposes. They do not envision a coming Rapture and many do not envision a coming Great Tribulation either, having sequestered the latter to the A.D. 70 event of Jerusalem's destruction. They are oblivious to the signs.

It is obvious that Satan on the other hand, *knows* the Rapture *will* occur. He knows the Great Tribulation will occur and it is for this event that he directs all of his energy, aggression, and power.

It is during this coming time of the greatest tribulation that this world will have ever experienced that Satan will reveal himself to the world through the Antichrist. He will first be seen as a kind, intelligent, loving, tolerant man who because of these things will rise to rule the entire world through a global government of Absolute Imperialism.

Though Satan is working toward the final showdown that will occur at the end of the Great Tribulation, it is also obvious that he does not know when either the Rapture or the Great Tribulation will actually occur. These times are in God's hands *only*. After that, the beginning of the Great Tribulation (comprising a *full* seven years), will start when the Antichrist is able to gain the trust of Israel, entering into a covenant with that nation for the seven years which make up the Tribulation/Great Tribulation.

 Ever watchful, Satan continues to keep tabs on everything that happens in this world that he has no control over. This allows him to judge the times and seasons, but as we have seen, though that is not enough, it is the best he can do.

Maitreya Clarifies...and Clarifies
Even when things are clarified by Maitreya or some other entity, as to *why*, for instance, the great planetary evacuation has not yet taken place, or why Maitreya himself has been unable to reveal himself, the blame is placed on those with *bad* energy.

Because these things are foretold to happen (as spoken of through various transmissions given over the space of twenty or thirty years), it is stated or implied that those who keep events from occurring are the *problem* people of this world. Instead of doubting Maitreya's power and ability, eyes turn instead to the *problem* (Christians) to see what can be done about that.

Even with this newest revelation from Crème himself regarding the alleged revealing of Maitreya (as posted on his website January 10, 2010), the only specifics presented by him were that Maitreya has "revealed" himself and that he has done so "as a man," and on an American talk show. Raj Patel, the assumed subject of Crème's announcement does not seem to share Crème's opinion, and was not specifically named by Crème.[31]

Of course, New Agers would say that it is very possible Patel does not yet *realize* that he is Maitreya at all, but that he will *grow* into that knowledge. The New Age always has a way of explaining things.

Since all fallen entities (including Nephilim) are under Satan's umbrella of evil, deception, *and* control, it makes sense that there is a constantly changing wind of doctrine within the body of New Age beliefs. In spite of this, all of it seems to continue to point to the one thing that Satan works toward.

What we know is that Satan as sole proprietor of the knowledge he himself has created and contained within the belief-system of the New Age, uses that knowledge at his discretion. He does so to advance his objectives and if that means using his minions (including the Nephilim) to progress and achieve his objectives, so be it.

Plus or Minus

Within the New Age Movement, the concept of *energy* – both positive and negative – is *foundational*. Those having a positive energy are enabled to move things forward to the next evolutionary phase. Those with a negative energy (Christians), keep things from happening the way the New Age adherents have been *told* they are *scheduled* to happen.

This of course, creates tension between the "world" (governed by Satan, under the sovereign eyes of God Himself), and Christ's kingdom and His followers. Most of the time, it is probably not even

---

[31] See Raj Patel's website at www.rajpatel.org , click on his Blog and search for "My Name is Brian"

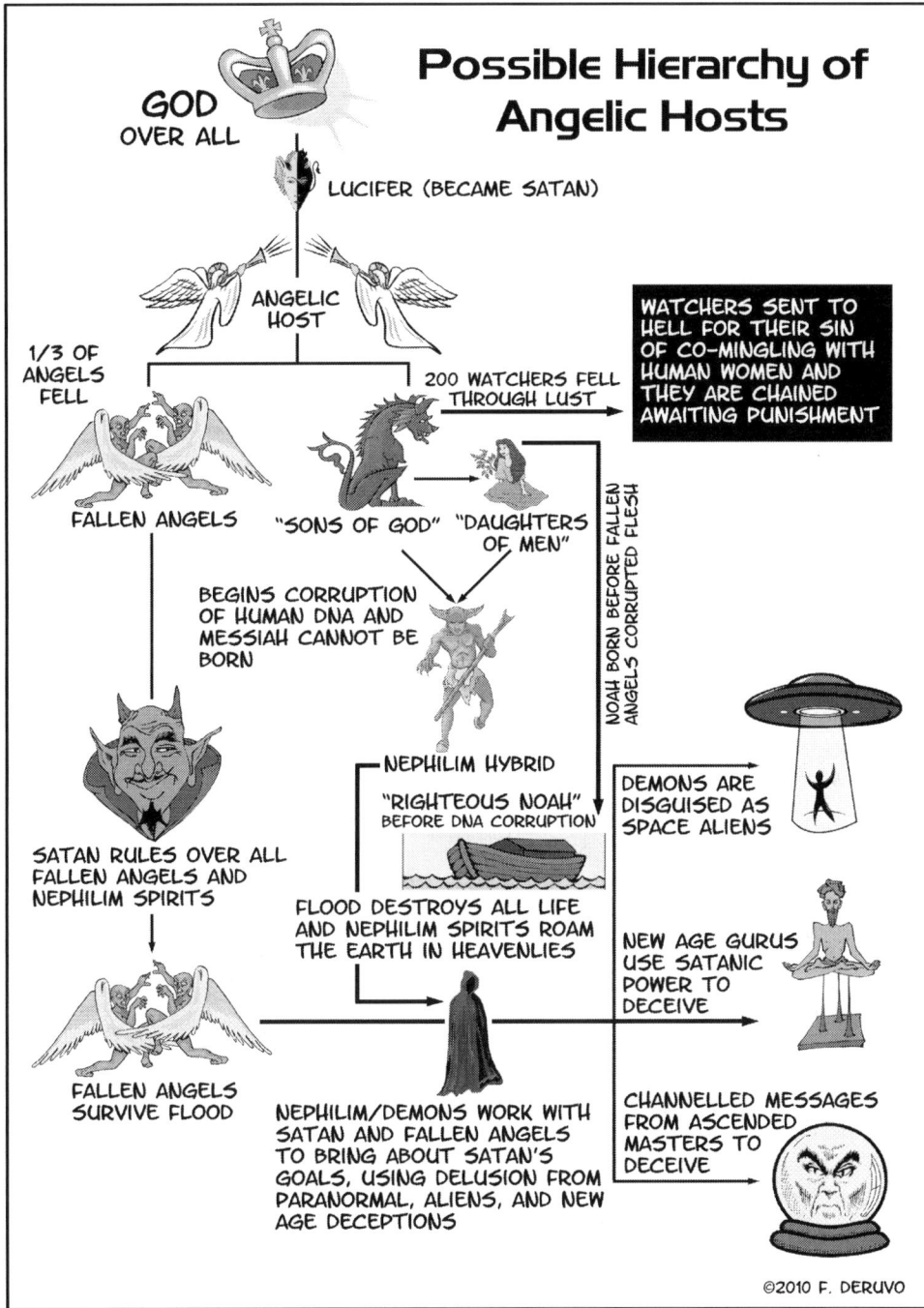

Possible Hierarchy of Angelic Hosts

GOD OVER ALL

LUCIFER (BECAME SATAN)

ANGELIC HOST

1/3 OF ANGELS FELL

200 WATCHERS FELL THROUGH LUST

WATCHERS SENT TO HELL FOR THEIR SIN OF CO-MINGLING WITH HUMAN WOMEN AND THEY ARE CHAINED AWAITING PUNISHMENT

FALLEN ANGELS

"SONS OF GOD"   "DAUGHTERS OF MEN"

BEGINS CORRUPTION OF HUMAN DNA AND MESSIAH CANNOT BE BORN

NOAH BORN BEFORE FALLEN ANGELS CORRUPTED FLESH

NEPHILIM HYBRID

SATAN RULES OVER ALL FALLEN ANGELS AND NEPHILIM SPIRITS

"RIGHTEOUS NOAH" BEFORE DNA CORRUPTION

DEMONS ARE DISGUISED AS SPACE ALIENS

FLOOD DESTROYS ALL LIFE AND NEPHILIM SPIRITS ROAM THE EARTH IN HEAVENLIES

NEW AGE GURUS USE SATANIC POWER TO DECEIVE

FALLEN ANGELS SURVIVE FLOOD

NEPHILIM/DEMONS WORK WITH SATAN AND FALLEN ANGELS TO BRING ABOUT SATAN'S GOALS, USING DELUSION FROM PARANORMAL, ALIENS, AND NEW AGE DECEPTIONS

CHANNELLED MESSAGES FROM ASCENDED MASTERS TO DECEIVE

©2010 F. DERUVO

understood *why* tension exists between authentic Christians and the world, yet it exists.

As I write this, I have experienced something that I have not experienced in some time. All of us have personality clashes. However, it is how we handle them that allows the light and truth of Christ to shine in and through us...or *not*.

Problems in the Spiritual Realm

I teach part-time at local junior colleges. I enjoy it immensely because I am only part-time, which eliminates from my schedule the amount of time spent in meetings and whatnot. Being a part-timer gives me a great deal of flexibility in my schedule. I also enjoy it because of the subjects I teach. Normally, these subjects incorporate aspects of MS Office® and we use these programs not only to teach the students *how* to use them, but at the same time, they are learning more about how to use *computers* in general.

This new quarter began a few weeks ago and everything was fine. However, one morning, one particular student took everything I said the wrong way. She became extremely argumentative and when I attempted to calmly defend myself, she accused me of "badgering" her and being "disrespectful." It was very weird. So I did what any teacher would do, by writing a narrative of the situation and including it in her record. I also forwarded the same record of the situation to my immediate supervisor.

Toward the end of that particular class period, one of the students dropped a note on my desk. It was a very nice, encouraging note, signed by two other students. I made a copy of it and gave that to my supervisor as well.

Frankly, the only reason I can assume that this person came unglued the way she did was because of something within the spiritual realm. I find no other reason for it.

My reaction to her has been one of love and compassion, just as Christ would respond to her. That has only occurred because by His grace, I have been able to submit myself constantly to Him. I cannot control *her* at all, though I have an obligation to submit myself to Him in order that His will might be accomplished in and through me.

I have come to realize that this problem began almost immediately after beginning to write this book. I did not realize it at the time and because of the oppression created by the powers of darkness (as allowed by God for my growth and His glory), my thinking was clouded. In fact, I discovered that writing this book became difficult. It was difficult to *concentrate*. I felt like I constantly had to readjust my focus, something I had not encountered in any of my previous books. Through concentrated prayer, the Lord got the message through that this was demonic activity and attack. It would not be surprising to discover that all Christians who write books on subjects like this experience greater attack.

It is likely that you have had similar experiences, which at first left you scratching your head wondering what you may have done to cause it. After you have searched and searched your brain for an answer, you are left with nothing that you can put your finger on. Through prayer and submission to Him, you come to the only possible conclusion that He has allowed Satan or one of his angels to test us, by creating a situation, which causes us to react. The way in which we react can and will determine whether our testimony is maintained or not.

We know that there is tension between God's coming Kingdom and Satan's dominion. Satan continues to work hard to achieve his goals and if/when he feels Christians get in the way, he does what he can to discourage us, or cause us to sin. God is also with us of course, and our responsibility at these times is to trust in His strength to be able to ride it out.

Besides working like this toward us, Satan seems to leave no group alone. He has carefully constructed a very complex plan and purpose so that every individual or group has their questions answered.

One day, as has been noted, according to New Age beliefs, space ships will park themselves above our skies, out of sight. Then, at the appointed time, they will literally vacuum the earth of that which keeps the planet and the people on it from entering a new phase of reality. Thus, the problem of earth's inability to rise to the next level of evolution will have been dealt with once and for all. Nothing then would continue to stand in the way of earth's advancement.

Where Will They Go?

What happens with all these millions of people who are instantly whisked away from the planet? We look again to Chuck Missler, who quotes from the spring 1994 issue of Connecting Link Magazine from an article written by Kay Wheeler.

Wheeler provides clarification on this upcoming event when millions in an instant will wind up missing. She states, "*Many of these beings who are leaving this planet at this time have completed that which they came to do. It is a time of great rejoicing for them. Do not feel sad about their leaving.* **They are going home.** *Many are waiting to be with them again…Many beings must move on, for their thought patterns are of the past. They hold on to these thoughts that keep Earth held back.*"[32] (emphasis added) Notice how Wheeler has *softened* the blow a bit here, yet at the same time what she is describing is the biblical event of *going home* (or dying).

She states that these individuals are holding the Earth back from its natural evolutionary advancement. She intones that these humans (referred to as "beings") are going to a better place. The world should experience a collective sigh of relief that those who held the

---

[32] Chuck Missler, *Alien Encounters* (Coeur d'Alene: Koinonia House 1997), 189

planet back are now gone, and it should also take solace in the fact that these missing people are going to a better place. Never let it be said that New Agers do not have "compassion."

Truth from a Liar?

I find all of this especially interesting, because *what* Wheeler is describing is exactly what Christians long for as we look to Christ for the fulfillment of it. In looking closely at what Wheeler has stated, there is a good deal of truth in it, *however* the beings that have revealed this information to Wheeler want her to understand not that the people Raptured off the planet are going to be with *Jesus*. He is not even mentioned at all. They want her to understand that this future event is all part of their specific *evolutionary path,* a path in which they will:

1.   *Rejoice*
2.   *Go home*
3.   *Be reunited with loved ones*

This is the perfect picture of what the Christian will experience once this life is completely over. We know that Satan is a liar and the hordes of demons who work out his will lie just as he lies, taking their cue from him. To *mix* truth with their lies is what comes naturally to them and if it brings about their chosen ends, all the better.

Satan goes on the offensive where the Rapture is concerned. Those within the church who deny that the Rapture is a biblical doctrine have obviously not been paying attention to what is going on *outside* the visible Church. While many are quarreling over meaning of passages of Scripture, they have missed a very large indicator that the Bible is *true.* Satan and his cohorts have spent decades telling lost people firmly established in the New Age Movement that such an event *would* occur. They have, however, given it their own special meaning.

The Rapture According to Satan

"professing themselves wise, they became as fools" Romans 1:22

FOR NEW AGERS:

People are being told that sometime in the future, an evacuation of millions of people will occur in the "twinkling of an eye." These people are said to keep the planet and its citizenry from evolving to the next level. Their removal means progression for the planet.

"scoffers will come in the last days" 2 Peter 3:3

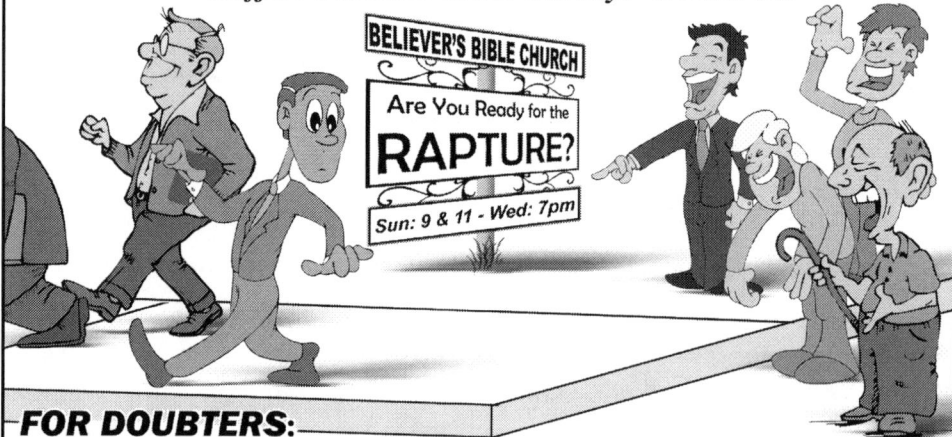

BELIEVER'S BIBLE CHURCH

Are You Ready for the

RAPTURE?

Sun: 9 & 11 - Wed: 7pm

FOR DOUBTERS:

These folks believe rumors like Margaret MacDonald started the Rapture story and Darby ran with it. Others believe that the Rapture was created by people who are merely looking for a persecution escape clause, or a fast way to make a quick buck.

The Rapture and the Second Coming

RAPTURE	SEVENTIETH WEEK OF DANIEL	SECOND ADVENT

RAPTURE PASSAGES

John 14:1-3	II Thessalonians 2:1
Romans 8:19	I Timothy 6:14
I Corinthians 1:7-8	I Timothy 4:1
I Corinthians 15:51-53	I Timothy 4:8
I Corinthians 16:22	Titus 2:13
Philippians 3:20-21	Hebrews 9:28
Philippians 4:5	James 5:7-9
Colossians 3:4	I Peter 1:7, 13
I Thessalonians 1:10	I Peter 5:4
I Thessalonians 2:19	I John 2:28-3:2
I Thessalonians 4:13-18	Jude 21
I Thessalonians 5:9	Revelation 2:25
I Thessalonians 5:23	

SECOND COMING PASSAGES

Daniel 2:44-45	Acts 19:11
Daniel 7:9-14	Acts 3:19-21
Daniel 12:1-3	I Thessalonians 3:13
Zechariah 14:1-15	I Peter 4:12-13
II Thessalonians 1:6-10	II Peter 3:1-14
Matthew 13:41	Jude 3:1-14
Matthew 24:15-31	Revelation 1:7
Matthew 26:64	
Mark 13:14-27	
Mark 14:62	
Revelation 19:11-20:6	
Luke 21:25-28	
Revelation 22:7, 12, 20	

15 Contrasting Events of the Second Coming

RAPTURE/BLESSED HOPE	GLORIOUS APPEARING
1) Christ comes in air for His own	1) Christ comes with His own to earth
2) Rapture/translation of all Christians	2) No one translated
3) Christians taken to Father's House	3) Resurrected saints do not see Father's House
4) No judgment on earth at Rapture	4) Christ judges inhabitants of earth
5) Church taken to Heaven at Rapture	5) Christ sets up His kingdom on earth
6) Rapture imminent	6) Glorious appearing cannot occur for 7 years
7) No signs for the Rapture	7) Many signs for Christ's physical coming
8) For believers only	8) Affects all humanity
9) Time of joy	9) Time of mourning
10) Before the Day of Wrath (Tribulation)	10) Immediately after Tribulation (Matthew 24)
11) No mention of Satan	11) Satan bound in Abyss for 1,000 years
12) The Judgment Seat of Christ	12) No time or place for Judgment Seat
13) Marriage of the Lamb	13) His bride descends with Him
14) Only His own see Him	14) Every eye will see Him
15) Tribulation can begin	15) 1,000-year kingdom of Christ begins

The question then regarding the possibility of the Rapture is simply this: *if the Rapture truly is a doctrine of devils with absolutely no biblical basis as some charge, then what <u>possible</u> reason would Satan have in creating any kind of deception surrounding it?*

If there is no chance of the Rapture occurring, why would he bother with it? It would be one thing to create a *false* teaching simply to confuse Christians and get them quarreling with one another. It is quite another thing altogether to teach *non-believers* that something like the Rapture *will* occur in the future. He has covered his bases.

Wasted Effort?

To create a scenario with this amount of detail, related to what will happen (but allegedly won't) creates a mystery to say the least. When the Rapture takes place, to non-believers and New Agers, it will be seen as something very good for them. They are already being trained to think that it is an event that *must* occur in order to allow this planet and citizens living here *after* the evacuation, to progress.

If the Rapture was *not* a possibility, it only stands to reason that Satan taking the time to create and explain it as an event planned by *him* would be counter-productive to his goals and purposes. Worse than that, it makes him appear as someone who really has no clue about what is happening, that is, if the Rapture was not in truth going to occur. Certainly, *he* would not be directly affected negatively, but his *plan* would and those through whom he is working and speaking would immediately lose at least some of their credibility.

It simply makes no sense for Satan to create such a charade based around an event that is *not* in the least biblical, unless he was only spending time attempting to prove to Christians that it was *not* going to happen. On the other hand, if the Rapture will occur, as I believe the Bible teaches, then Satan has an excellent reason to create a diversion by teaching that what will be happening is not a *biblical* event, but one that has to do with the earth's advancement on the evolutionary timeline.

The Rapture is a biblical event, in my opinion. To me, it is clear not only from Scripture, but also from what the enemy of our souls is telling those who are currently caught in his web of his lies and deceit. The last thing Satan wants the average, unsaved person to know is the truth concerning the Rapture (or any part of the Bible). That will not do at all. Better they see this upcoming event as something *he* designed (through those appearing as *aliens,* and *ascended masters*), for the good of this planet and the good of humanity. He gains much by also having Christians come to disbelieve in the veracity of the Rapture doctrine.

The charts on the previous pages highlight passages referring to the Rapture and Second Coming (based on Fruchtenbaum's book *Footsteps of the Messiah*). The top chart compares passages of Scripture connected with the Second Coming to those connected with the Rapture. The bottom chart compares and contrasts the events themselves and as can be seen, there are many differences between these two events.

The reader is encouraged to study the various sections of Scripture listed in each on their own, to determine exactly what these differences are between the two events. Beyond this, for a complete detailing of these two events, the aforementioned book by Dr. Fruchtenbaum is a must for anyone's library.

The following chart (also based on Fruchtenbaum's book Footsteps of the Messiah), outlines the Promise of the Rapture, the Program of the Rapture and the Timing of the Rapture. The clear teaching of Scripture designates a specific event in which all who are in Christ (the Church), are *translated*, or *caught up* to be with Him in the clouds. This event, unlike the Second Coming, is *not* a return of Christ to earth. In this event, He merely steps away from His throne, out of the third heaven and greets His Bride as His Bride is translated to Him, after He calls them.

This event is also very similar to the way Enoch was translated prior to the judgment of the global flood in Genesis 4. Enoch walked with God and *"was not because the Lord took him."* Enoch then, was removed from this earth while still *alive*. He did not see death. This is the exact sense in which Christ's Bride, having already been purified due to His shed blood on Calvary's cross, is caught up to be with Him forever.

Isn't the Church Already Purified?

Many people today teach that the Church needs to be purified *before* we are able to be presented to Him blameless. This is a false teaching. Paul teaches that there is therefore now NO condemnation to those who are in Christ Jesus (Romans 8:1). For the Christian, there should be no fear in standing before Jesus Christ in judgment with respect to our *salvation*. Depending upon how we have chosen to live our lives after we have received salvation, will determine the

Promise of the Rapture	Program of the Rapture	Timing of the Rapture
JOHN 14:1-3 Jesus will receive us to Himself.	2 THESSALONIANS 4:13-18 Believers who have died will rise first and then those who are still alive.	1. THE CHURCH AND THE TRIBULATION • No biblical passage which discusses the Tribulation mentions the Church. 2. PRETRIBULATIONAL RAPTURE • LUKE 21:34-37 is the earliest indication of teaching. 3. PRETRIBULATIONAL DELIVERANCE • Taught in 1 THESSALONIANS 4:13-18 • the closing words are crucial ~ "wrath to come." • the wrath is future; not sin in general • the wrath refers to the Great Tribulation 4. CHURCH NOT APPOINTED TO WRATH • 1 THESSAONLIANS 5:1-10 says this (which points back to the Day of the Lord phrase). 5. RAPTURE IS IMMINENT • Scriptures teach this - and that it precedes the Great Tribulation.

pages 142-154 in Footsteps

rewards (if any) we will receive *beyond* salvation. This takes place at the Bema Judgment Seat of Christ for the believer. I have actually begun another book on this very subject. Stay tuned.

The Church Awaits for the Last Gentile

The Church awaits the fullness of the Gentiles (cf. Romans 11), which is the time we are now living. During this phase, God continues to call out those earmarked for salvation from *every* nation and culture. When the last of these has been called out, the fullness of the Gentiles will have been reached.

In a day and age when people balk at the doctrine of the Rapture, or of His return, it is important to honestly understand what the *Bible* teaches. Is the Rapture grounded doctrinally in His Word, or is it a figment of someone's overworked imagination?

Because of what the New Age teaches throughout its loose knit network of adherents, it would appear that Satan *knows* the Rapture will occur. It is because of this that he has taken the time to thoroughly indoctrinate his followers with the truth of the Rapture, *albeit* with his own special version. It unquestionably seems to be working.

Chapter 6

Demonic Infiltration

As we saw in our previous chapter, Satan has been busy pulling the wool over the eyes of his own human followers, both in and out of the visible Church using various distorted views of doctrines such as the Rapture. In this chapter, we will take the time to detail a few more of the overall teachings that Satan and his minions have been expertly weaving into the fabric of society so that they have become not only common, but also commonly *accepted*. In order for Satan's long-term plan to work, he must cover all of his bases.

In his book *Alien Encounter,* Chuck Missler explains how the New Age Movement began in the United States. It essentially stemmed from the writings of Helena Blavatsky, who lived in the middle to late 1800s, and whose articles gave rise to the Theosophical Society. Her many writings prompted other individuals like Alice Bailey and sci-fi writer H.G. Wells to pick up and carry her motif, if not her work, forward.

While many would deny the New Age Movement is an actual *religion,* in many ways, it *is* a religion, albeit one, that defies certain definitions. People do not necessarily meet weekly in a house of worship, but they do have their own bible of sorts. One of the main books they look to is called *Oahspe: The Aquarian Gospel of Jesus the Christ; My Truth, the Lord Himself;* and *My Peace, the Lord Himself;* this according to Missler.

Relaxed Focus

What ties New Age adherents together is their *belief system.* The *one* main belief that they share is, as Missler points out, "the Source" or "the God of Force." Essentially, those within the New Age Movement believe that man is essentially *divine.* God already *resides* within everyone. It is no coincidence that most aliens teach variants of this same doctrine. The problem is that most of us are simply not aware of this fact. The New Age provides the deep or secret *knowledge,* which helps people *become* aware of their own inner divinity.

This is accomplished through numerous methods, but chief among them is *meditation.* Meditation occurs when people enter into a state of *relaxed focus,* for the lack of a better phrase. This relaxed focus allows the practitioner's mind to go on *pause*, in order to *hear* from those within the spirit world. Relaxed focus opens the door to these entities, along with any false messages they wish to transmit.

Interestingly enough, this is not at all different from that promoted within the Emergent Church, such as *Contemplative Prayer.* In this practice, the Christian is encouraged to arrive at this same state, in order that God might speak to the inner man. What actually happens is the same thing that occurs in the brain of a New Ager. Once the brain goes into pause mode, the alpha waves take over creating an *alternate* state. In this alternate state, messages can be received from those from *outside* the individual's mind. Under normal conditions, when our mind is *actively thinking* (even though we do not notice that we are concentrating or thinking), it is very difficult, if not impossible for these messages to get through to us. People have to be *open* to them. This is also why people who have taken drugs like LSD and other hallucinogens claim to have "seen" God. Once the alpha wave state is reached, anything *can* and *will* come into fill the void that this state creates. In fact, this is exactly what the powers of darkness *need* to gain access to an individual, ultimately resulting in *oppression*, or *possession*. The door needs to open to them, and when the brain is *stilled* through meditation, the door opens *wide*.

Again and Again
The cycle of reincarnation is also a commonly taught principle within New Age. By the way, it should be noted that *all* religious beliefs are allowed and *encouraged* within the New Age arena, all with the *exception* of <u>Christianity</u>. Jesus Christ is only spoken of in terms of an impersonal consciousness, or a *collective* of entities or energies. He is not a Person specifically, but a *level* to which a person ascends.

Regarding reincarnation, each newly recycled life brings the adherent another opportunity to become more and more aware of his or her own divinity (this is the *hoped* for scenario), until eventually no further reincarnations are required. The person will have at that point, come to a *full* recognition of their own inner divinity and will have full control over their own life with the ability to create their own reality.

Many New Agers believe that this perfectly describes Jesus, whom they believe, was merely a man, though developed an underlying awareness of His own inner divinity. Over the course of His life, Jesus is said to have applied the principles of reincarnation to achieve *oneness*. At this point, He learned to create His own reality.

Should the person *not* make any headway with their newest reincarnation, they end up moving backwards, with *more* future reincarnations necessary in order to actualize their full *divinity*. While it was extremely unusual to hear people talk of "past lives" a few decades ago, this is not the case today. It is now common water cooler conversation; something accepted by many to most in today's world.

Whether all who speak of reincarnation truly believe it, is something else entirely. However, it has become widely accepted to discuss it openly without fear of ridicule. In fact, *because* of the plurality of eastern cultures which have grown exponentially over the last twenty or thirty years, talk *of*, and belief *in* reincarnation has become quite acceptable and encouraged, while the New Age itself is heavily promoted through it.

Often within the context of the New Age movement, the phrase "Christ Consciousness" is used to define a particular *office* or *level of ascendency*. The Christ Consciousness then is *not* one particular individual, but something that all can (and should) achieve. In this regard, the man Jesus was One who *became*, over His lifetime an individual, who fully embraced the Christ Consciousness that was already resident within Him, though initially *dormant*. This, in effect, is what enabled Him to do all the things that He did while He lived on this earth, many of which only *appeared* to be miraculous to us. This is the believed and expected norm for *all* people to embrace.

Salvation: the Office of <u>Being</u> Christ for Each of Us

It was the office of the Christ Consciousness that provided Jesus with all of His ability. Apart from this, He was a human being, as all of us are human beings. Jesus then, worked diligently throughout His life to attain that level of ascendency. For the New Age person, this then is what they would call *salvation*. One works very hard, conscientiously trying to become *one with the universe*, in order to *actualize* the divinity that already lies inactive within each person. Once having achieved that level, the *hard* work is over and the person becomes an *ascended master*, turning to help others who have not yet arrived. In essence, then, those within the New Age movement and Maitreya himself *deny* that Jesus Christ actually came in the flesh (cf. 1 John 4:1-3). Though Jesus was born on this planet growing to understand the divinity within Him, He did not *arrive* on this planet *as God* from the start. This view, and all who hold it, is the view of the Antichrist (cf. 2 John 1:7).

Missler outlines the goals of the New Age movement. *"They share the goal of creating a world peace through unification in a one-world spiritual system and a one-world government through a one-world leader of their choosing. Their covert goals are to abolish all systems based on the Bible by the year 2000, which is the beginning of the Age of Aquarius. They endeavor to convert Western religious and philosophical belief systems into those of Eastern thought."*[33]

What this means of course, is that the way is being paved for a one-world *government* in which *one* individual will become *supreme* ruler, enforcing a one-world *religion* as well. Ultimately, this one-world religion will segue into the worship of this coming dictator, who will rule as an Absolute Imperialist (as Fruchtenbaum states in his book, *Footsteps of the Messiah*).

Sounds Like Science Fiction

It is certainly interesting to think about all the sci-fi movies, TV series and the like, which deal with some maniacal, brilliant megalomaniac whose goal is to rule the world. Most of the world views those programs as merely Hollywood's fascination with the science fiction genre. It is easy to realize that since time immemorial, movies dedicated to Satan have existed. Who can think of a time they did not

---

[33] Chuck Missler, *Alien Encounters* (Coeur d'Alene: Koinonia House 1997), 144

exist, beginning with some of the first silent films? I firmly believe that these movies have played a strong part in advancing the beliefs of New Age, Satanism, and demonology. While many of these movies appeared mild compared to that which exists today, they served a purpose, and that purpose was to allow people to become used to the concept of Satan and demons.

Not found merely in films either, radio played a very important part in the release of ideas into our society. Can anyone forget "War of the Worlds," a radio program hosted by Orson Wells, in which aliens were said to have attacked earth (1938). The radio program provided a play-by-play for listeners and panic ensued. Since the technology then was nothing like it is today, news crews were unable to get to the scene to ascertain the truth of the situation, as they would today. People simply *assumed* it was all true. Some committed suicide, while many tried to get out of New Jersey, where the "attack" was allegedly occurring. This opened the door to other things that followed.

Classic films like *The Wolfman, Frankenstein, Dracula*, and others shocked and terrified audiences when they first came out. Compared to today, these movies are very tame.

Modeling Monsters

I recall when I was a kid, the Aurora Plastics Corporation spent months and months agonizing over whether or not to produce figure model kits based on the main characters of these horror movies. The top brass at Aurora were opposed to it, yet one high up individual really pushed for it. They finally did a test market and the results were overwhelmingly in favor of producing these models. The first horror model Aurora produced was *Frankenstein*, and once the model hit the shelves, Aurora was unable to keep up with the demand.

The executives at Aurora realized then that they had a major hit on their hands. This kit not only catapulted them into an entire line of horror monster models, but also pushed open the door for *other* companies to manufacture their own horror models. Soon, Aurora had produced, *Dracula, Wolfman, Godzilla, Creature from the Black Lagoon, King Kong* and numerous other horror-related models for young boys.

Building model kits had become a growing phenomenon overnight when Aurora made the decision to produce Frankenstein. Demand for the model increased to such a point that required Aurora to operate their injection-molding machines round the clock and they *still* had to create three more sets of molds for subcontractors.

Soon, other companies like Revell and Monogram got into the act, producing horror model kits of their own. Young boys could not get enough, running to the store on a near-weekly basis to purchase the latest model kit, which had just hit the shelves.

This of course created a cycle of models based on other movie characters, and then magazines like *Famous Monsters of Filmland* became the staple of the day for horror fans not into building models. However, there was a good deal of crossover because often, model builders read the magazines and vice versa.

Though the figure model craze began to die in the mid-seventies, it came back full force in the late 1980s and into the 90s. The very same models were reissued once again.

Unfortunately, these later decades were not like the 1960s and 70s. The horror models now being produced (separate from the more tame classic monsters), were by far more *gruesome*, leaving little to the imagination. It seemed like the bloodier, the better. The tragic part is that a number of these model kits reflected real-life criminals and events. Figure kits of *Ed Gein* (serial killer and grave robber of the 1950s), *Jack the Ripper, Marquis de Sade*, and even one of *O. J. Simpson* represented as the murderer of his ex-wife and Ronald Goldman. The description of the model needs not be included here.

GHOSTLY GLOW-POWER STRIKES!
THE MONSTERS ARE BACK, AND THEY GLOW IN THE DARK.
AURORA
FAMOUS
MONSTERS
OF FILMLAND
WHO WAS THE MAN WHO
LOST HIS FACE
?
... SEE PAGE 18
UNIVERSAL PICTURES PRESENTS
THE BRIDE OF FRANKENSTEIN
ALL-PLASTIC ASSEMBLY KIT
MOEBIUS MONSTER SCENES
ALL PLASTIC SNAP TOGETHER CUSTOM BUILDER KITS
DR. DEADLY
MAKE A FRIEND!
BUILD "BIG FRANKIE"
THE FRIENDLIEST MONSTER IN TOWN!
FRANKENSTEIN
AURORA
AURORA
TOHO PRODUCTIONS PRESENTS
GODZILLA
ALL PLASTIC ASSEMBLY KIT
AURORA
UFO
FROM
THE INVADERS
ALL PLASTIC ASSEMBLY KIT
COCKPIT COVER REMOVED —
The PHANTOM of the OPERA

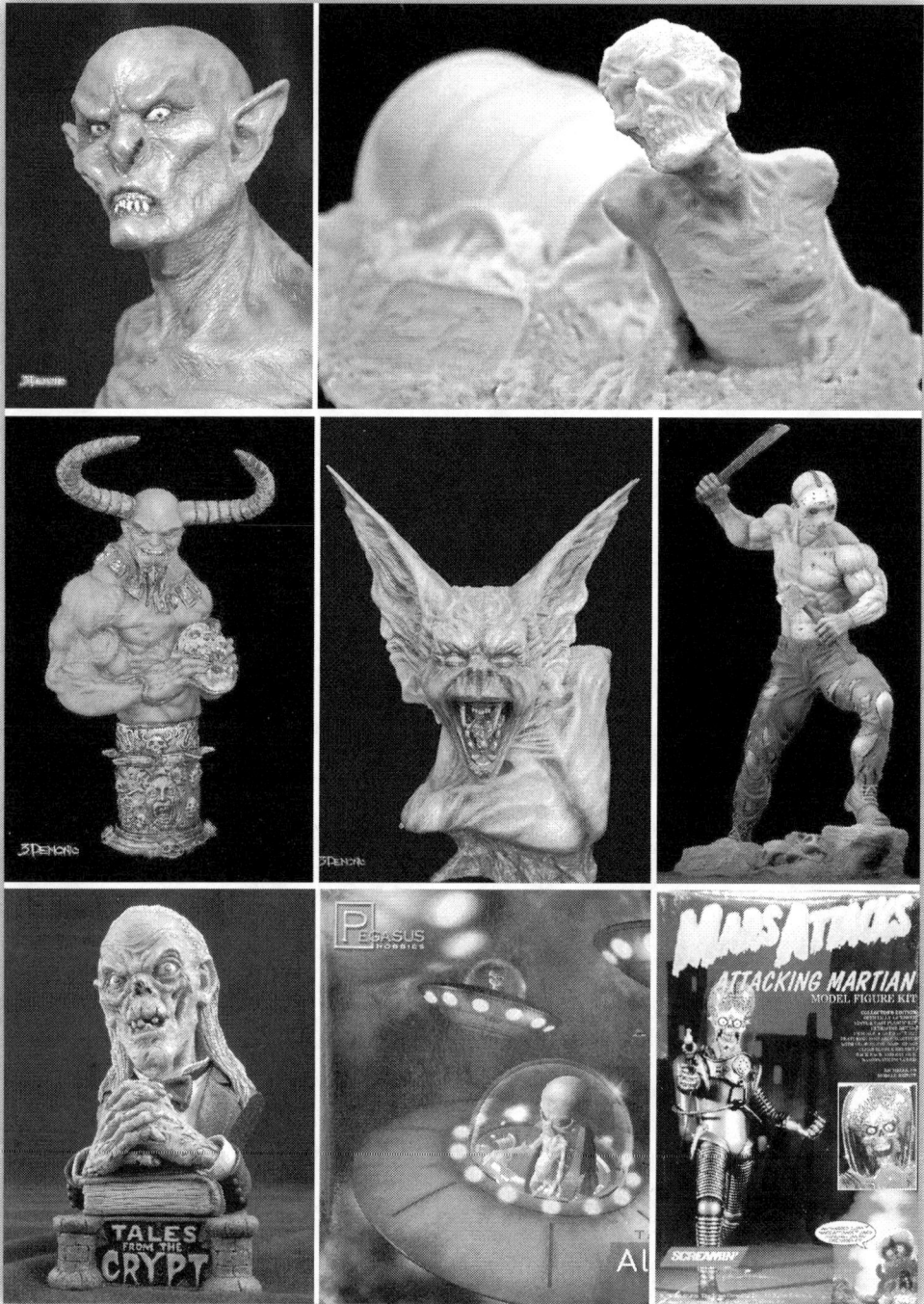

One of the other things that came to the fore through this resurrected modeling hobby deals with images of demons and even Satan himself! Since the 1960s and 70s, more and more movies had been produced dealing with aspects of the occult. Movies like The Omen, Rosemary's Baby, and others opened the gateway for more movies, which were far more gruesome. The now classic movie, *The Exorcist*, starring Linda Blair dealt strongly with the occult, with the devil nearly winning in the end. In some ways, the devil did win because he was able to overcome in one way or other those who came to cast him out of the girl, Regan.

Friday the 13th, *Halloween* and *A Nightmare on Elm Street*, all became mainstays of the movie industry whose characters are well known to most people today. Freddy Krueger, Jason and others are known for their paranormal bloodlust. The scarier and more gruesome each move became, the more audiences yelled for more, much more. Movie studios obliged because of the almighty dollar.

Of course, it was not long before model companies decided that they also wanted to cash in on the newest horror craze and did so, producing models based on the many of the current movies of the day.

There seemed to be no end in sight and even today, part of the modeling community continues to exist. Their favorite models are ones that have anything to do with horror and nude women. Modeling companies cash in *twice* by producing a model of a *nude* woman in a *horror* scene. Many of these models sell for $100 plus, produced in resin, or cold cast porcelain!

Go Figure
All of this began with Aurora's decision to produce *Frankenstein*. This opened the floodgates and that one decision has brought us to the point where we are today, and there is no going back. What began as seemingly innocuous has become anything *but* that.

The photos on page 106 show model kits and busts produced by *today's* modeling companies. As can be seen, the subjects of these models range from occult and demonic to alien. The bust shown in the middle row, far left, is actually called *Lucifer* and is produced by a company called 3Demonic. The Mars Attacks kit (lower right), was an authorized model based on the characters, which were turned into a movie. There was an entire series of these *Mars Attacks* kits, some of which incorporated not only dead humans, but also humans who had literally been *slaughtered* by alien intruders. It seemed the bloodier, the better the model sold.

However, of late, more and more reading material and movies are being produced about Satan. Movies have come a very long way, since the horror movies of the 40s, 50s, and 60s. Movies like Mars Attacks, Men in Black, and other big budget movies were done with a tongue-in-cheek style, allowing the audience to laugh at the situation, while being grossed out at the same time.

Other movies like the aforementioned A Nightmare on Elm Street, Halloween, and Friday the 13th went full bore on the gore, leaving nothing to the imagination. This has created a society that is

becoming *obsessed with* but *numb* to the forces of darkness. Society routinely accepts these characters as far-fetched, over-the-top. However, not all movies are produced this way. At least some of the movies that have been produced and are being produced as this book is written, present a much more "realistic" approach to the occult, Satan, and gore. The idea here is for the audience to come away believing that what they see in these movies could actually happen, and may very well be happening *now*, right under our noses.

One such movie is being produced by Ray Griggs is simply called *Lucifer*. Mr. Griggs has produced a *short*, or mini-version of part of the movie, which allows potential investors to see what the final movie may look like. As soon as I saw the short, I realized that what was being taught in the movie presents some of the doctrine of Mormonism. It is that Lucifer was equal to Jesus, yet Lucifer wound up falling from grace and become Satan. I sent an email to Griggs asking if the background of the movie was based on Mormonism and whether or not he himself is a Mormon. To date, no response has been received.

Interestingly enough, according to Griggs, many *Christians* are actually excited to know that the movie is in production and cannot wait until they can view it. In an interview from December 2008, when asked what the movie was about, Griggs responded with, "*This is the story of an exalted angel, charismatic, even heroic, who sat at the right hand of God presumed to be the "chosen one" to rule the Kingdom of Heaven. But this angel whose fierce pride fueled an ambition that would corrupt his judgment, alienate him from his closest friend, divide the heavenly host into two warring factions, and ultimately bring Sin and Death to mankind. This story is the first of a trilogy concerning the greatest epic battle since Creation. It's the fall of Lucifer, Satan, the Prince of Darkness.*"[34]

---

[34] http://fantasy-films.suite101.com/article.cfm/lucifer_the_movie

When asked what type of reaction he had received so far, based on the short he had produced, Griggs stated, *"It's not just from a Christian group, it's all groups who have left wonderful comments on the website. I've had atheists want to see this film and Jews want to see it. That's what's really amazing because it's a film that many different people want to see and want to be in line for. I've had nice compliments that they could see it as a trilogy like Lord of the Rings and that's really honorable."*[35]

Beyond this movie, there are others and as I write this, one movie has been released, concentrating on Michael, the Archangel. He comes to earth to save a woman who is carry a baby, *the* baby that will apparently save the world.

This movie, called *Legion*, boasts this plot: *"When God loses faith in humankind, he sends his legion of angels to bring on the Apocalypse. Humanity's only hope lies in a group of strangers trapped in a desert diner with the Archangel Michael."*[36]

Lucifer is "Funny" Stuff

A comic book, which has been around for a while is *Lucifer*. This comic book grew out of *The Sandman* series and took on a life of its own. One blogger stated this about the comic book series, *"The theme of the Lucifer series revolves around the free will problem. Carey's Lucifer is a Nietzschean figure representing will and individual willpower, who challenges the 'tyranny of predestination'. While in heaven's eyes this is blasphemy, Lucifer points out that rebellion (and indeed all sin) and damnation as consequence were pre-planned by his Creator. Lucifer rejects God's rule as tyrannical and unjust. Violent, aggressive, vengeful, and dictatorial aspects of heaven's rule are represented by the archangel Amenadiel, who has a particular hatred of Lucifer and leads attacks of various kinds against him, such as verbal*

---

[35] http://fantasy-films.suite101.com/article.cfm/lucifer_the_movie
[36] http://www.imdb.com/title/tt1038686/plotsummary

criticism, marshalling the host of heaven as well as challenging him to individual combat. For his part, Lucifer disdains Amenadiel, treating his emotional outbursts with contempt and repeatedly defeating his assaults with Machiavellian scheming."[37]

Speak to anyone who has been an adherent of the New Age movement for any length of time, and while they might balk at the idea of a one-world ruler, they *do* look forward to a time of perpetual peace, which many believe will only occur *through* one individual.

What should be easy for any true Christian to see is that all of this leads to the *climax* of what Satan has *wished* for, *worked* for and *believed* he would *gain*, since he fell out of favor with God. He has always wanted to be *better* than the Most High. This prideful arrogance caused his fall from the high position he once held. In fact, of all the *created* beings, Satan as Lucifer was the highest and it is from that lofty height he fell, (cf. Isaiah 14:12-14; Ezekiel 28:12-20; Revelation 12:7-12).

Satan has never given up on his desire to not only be *like* the Most High, but to be *worshipped* as God is worshipped. Everything he has done in the past, continues to do in the present, and works toward in the future sees its culmination in this one goal. He longs to be worshipped as God is worshipped. He wants all of God's Creation to direct their gaze with adoring love and praise in *his* direction, ignoring God altogether, yet Satan is a *created* being!

Daniel, Ezekiel, and *Revelation* teach us that Satan *will* have this, but only for a short time. This will be accomplished through the man he raises up of whom the Bible calls the *man of sin, man of lawlessness*, the *Beast* and other titles as well.

Though we are seeing more from Hollywood and the comic book industry, in their attempts to make Lucifer more *human*, more

---

[37] http://en.wikipedia.org/wiki/Lucifer_(DC_Comics)

recognizable as a unique individual, and no longer a cartoon, it remains that the New Age movement has been and continues to be the primary vehicle in preparing the world for this man. It is also obvious that the New Age movement has extended itself into areas of entertainment more than ever before.

The New Age movement is ushering in the day when the world will truly be *one*, under the barbaric leadership of this man of sin. Completely overtaken by Satan, the Antichrist will set himself up as god halfway through the Tribulation. People worshipping him will in fact be bowing to *Satan*.

Because Antichrist breaks his covenant with Israel (that he instituted at the beginning of the Tribulation) halfway through the Tribulation, allowing Israel to finally realize what has happened, they head for the hills, literally. Antichrist's resultant terror will become fully unleashed and thus begins the Great Tribulation, which is the final three and a half years of man-led human history. This period will end with the physical return of Jesus Christ Himself.

Constance Cumby Weighs In

Constance Cumby has authored a number of books on the subject of the New Age. In many respects, she is considered an expert in the field of New Age. Her book *The Hidden Dangers of the Rainbow* begins with this ominous outlook:

"It is the contention of this writer that for the first time in history there is a viable movement – the New Age Movement – that truly meets all the scriptural requirements for the antichrist and the political movement that will bring him on the world scene.

"It is further the position of the writer that this most likely is the great apostasy or 'falling away' spoken of by the Apostle Paul and that the

antichrist's appearance could be a very real event in our immediate future."[38]

Cumby wrote those words in 1983, and what she says certainly sounds ominous. Isn't the New Age movement merely made up of people who *meditate* and do *Tai Chi*, or something similar? Aren't they all merely *harmless* vegetarians, who are trying to find ways to relax and be at peace within? All evidence would seem to say while many *believe* this to be the case (especially among the adherents) the New Age movement is much more than this.

Cumby confirms that within the New Age movement, the name of Maitreya is extremely important. It represents *not* a man, but a fifth reincarnation of Buddha, one who will take over the reins with his appearing to *create* a new world order. This in itself may be at least *part* of the reason there are believed to be *two* individuals referred to as Maitreya now. One is the aforementioned Raj Patel associated with Benjamin Crème. Not surprisingly, the other Maitreya that Cumby highlights believes the Crème Maitreya to be an imposter and that Crème himself is inwardly a dragon.

Maitreya's Mission

Cumby indicates, "*Maitreya's followers are now in the last stage of the New Age scheme to take the world for Lucifer. Lucis Trust - formerly Lucifer Trust – ran ads in the* Reader's Digest, *which displayed The Great Invocation to Maitreya. The Great Invocation refers to The Plan. It says, 'Let Light and Love and Power restore the Plan on Earth'.*"[39]

Cumby's explanation of *The Plan* turns out to be nothing less than a Messiah for the new world he will establish, complete with a new government along with a new, one-world religion. The website of the

---

[38] Constance Cumby, *The Hidden Dangers of the Rainbow* (Shreveport: Huntington House 1983), 7
[39] Ibid, 7

individual Cumby refers to, contains a map of how The Plan looks and how it will work itself out.[40]

Cumby also mentions one of the websites dedicated to Maitreya called *Mission of Maitreya*. Visiting the site introduces visitors to the teachings of Maitreya as well as statements like this: "*By entering this website, you are about to find the most amazing Truth. Humanity has been waiting for this Revelation for the last twelve thousand years.*"[41]

The front page of this site continues by declaring that all major religions are really *one* in the same. "*In fact they are complementary and were sent to earth systematically by One God. When this is understood, the Path to Salvation (Eternal Divine Path) is known!*"[42]

The site unashamedly declares "*The Goal Of Life Is To Be(come) Divine, That Divinity (God) Is Everything.*"[43] This is the *keynote* address and main pursuit of the entire New Age movement. Perusing the site shows just how Christianity is viewed by these folks and by this Maitreya himself.

As usual, with much of the information found on the site in the form of teaching, it is a mix of actual Scripture, though conveniently twisted to mean something other than what it actually means. While denying that he is the Antichrist, this Maitreya claims to be the last prophet of God to humanity.

This is clearly stated in the *Letter to Leaders* posted on the website, with the title *God is Calling You (The Last Call)*, dated March 2, 2007. "*As Prophet Noah warned people in his time of the forthcoming flood, and Prophet Jonah warned the people of Nineveh of the coming disaster to their city, this is a warning from the Prophet of God (Maitreya) to*

---

[40] http://www.maitreya.org/files/Plan/themap.htm
[41] http://www.maitreya.org/ 06/09/2009
[42] Ibid
[43] http://www.maitreya.org/english/third_eye.htm 06/09/2009

humanity of the imminent disasters predicted to come at the end time!"[44]

The letter continues, affirming the oneness of all major religions, *"There is no separation between religions, and there is only One God for the whole of humanity. Understanding how each of the world's religions have come in perfect order, and how each have an important part (Message) for mankind, is now revealed to man."*[45]

As expected, this Maitreya insists his lineage goes back not only to King David, but to Muhammad as well, and from this, he claims connection to the Hebrew race and the Lion of Judah. This Maitreya has been here since 1977, and is waiting for the proper time to reveal himself to the world as the Messiah. There is that "proper time" problem again. At the same time, one wonders, is he not *already* revealing himself on his website now?

As if the news about Maitreya(s) is not enough, there is at least one man on the Internet who claims to be one of the two witnesses seen in the book of Revelation. He states on his website (in part), *"As God has made me both an apostle and a prophet for this end-time, He has also given me to fulfill prophecies being the spokesman of the two end-time witnesses of Revelation 11. In addition, He has given me to fulfill the prophecies of the "Elijah to come" and of Zerubbabel. It is actually God, in and through Jesus Christ, who fulfills all these things, but He is doing so through a human instrument. The Book of Acts makes it very clear that Jesus Christ will come to fully restore all things in God's great plan after He returns in his second coming as King of kings."*[46]

The man in question is Ronald Weinland, a follower of Herbert W. Armstrong. He does not believe that either John the Baptist or

---

[44] http://www.maitreya.org/english/Letters/Leaders/letter_to_leaders.htm 06/09/2009
[45] Ibid
[46] http://www.ronaldweinland.com/

Armstrong himself fulfilled the necessary requirements or prophecies for the Elijah who is to come. He firmly believes he is the one who will do that, in God's strength and power. He has no idea who the other "witness" of Revelation 11 is, but he is convinced that he is one of them. So, the delusions continue.

"It Already Happened!"
What is truly amazing is the fact that though many within the church *deny* a number of aspects of biblical prophecy, others assume things about these prophecies that are merely imagined. As we have just seen, Weinland believes himself to be one of the witnesses of Revelation 11. To read his Blog is to enter into a world of imagination and fabrication.

On the other hand, doctrines such as the literal Second Coming of Jesus, and a literal Antichrist who is to precede Him, are routinely rejected. Instead, what is believed to occur is a *continuation* of Christ's *spiritual* return, in contrast to a *literal*. The Antichrist is not a *person*, but an *attitude*. Some *do* believe in an actual Antichrist, but many of these also believe he has come and gone in the form of Nero, the infamous Roman Emperor, or some other Roman Caesar.

Many believe the return of Christ occurred in A.D. 70, with the destruction of Jerusalem and the Temple that was *then* standing. Of course, this return of Christ is said to have been *spiritual* in nature, not physical. This is in spite of the testimony of the two angels in Acts 1, who informed the disciples (who had just seen Christ ascending into heaven), that this same Jesus would return in *the same way* they had seen Him go. It is natural and reasonable to believe that the angels meant that He would return *physically*. In spite of the obviousness of the passage, people continue to adopt an allegorical approach in understanding of text.

We are told in Revelation 1:7 that Jesus *is* going to return, and He will return on the clouds and *every eye shall see Him*. What else could this

116

possibly mean than He will *physically* return and everyone will see Him because they will look up, and there He will be, arriving on the clouds? With the advent of satellite, cable TV, the Internet, and other media, it will be *impossible* to miss that event.

From the perspective of the New Age movement, they believe that one specific individual will appear to usher in the final age, which essentially becomes the new age. This *new* age, as has been stated, includes a one-world government and a one-world religion, headed up by this one man, of whom the unsaved world will eventually worship.

The Emergent Church is right there alongside the New Age movement, believing that their work will usher in a postmodern version of Christianity, which is nothing more than a *social* gospel. Both leaders and adherents of the Emergent Church see Christianity as working to help people physically, as opposed to spiritually. Of course, they deny this, because they also believe that by teaching people how to "make and keep friends," "live their best life now," and other platitudes, spiritual needs of people *are* being met. People like Tony Campolo, Brian McLaren, Joel Osteen, Rick Warren, and others have intimated, implied, or stated that one is not even required to be a Christian in order to actually have salvation.

Satan Knows the Bible Better Than We Do

Now of course the question must be asked, if the references to the Rapture, *the* Antichrist and any type of Tribulation/Great Tribulation are not real, then *why* is Satan even bothering to teach his version of these doctrines to New Age proponents? Satan *appears* to be working diligently to bring something about that has no basis in biblical fact, and will not occur (if conservative biblical scholarship is *wrong*). Why bother creating this entire façade if there is no chance of it occurring?

Satan knows the Bible, and he knows it better than anyone on this planet does. He also has a much better *vantage* point to see what God is actually doing because he exists in *that* dimension. Our vantage point requires a good deal of *faith* because we are unable to see that realm as part of the natural course of our lives. Satan actually *sees* things in the *making*. He hears what the discussions and sees the results of those discussions. While he is unable to be everywhere at once and certainly does not know everything, he has a better *actual* picture of what is happening throughout the world *now* largely, because he guides much of it, *with* God's permission.

The point is that Satan knows what the Bible *says* and what it *teaches*. He certainly understands the meaning of major prophetic utterances in Scripture, especially when they concern *him*. He *knows* that the Bible teaches the Rapture as previously pointed out, and he is well aware of the fact that Jesus *is* going to return physically to this planet. Jesus *will* return to *judge* and set up His *kingdom*, from which He will reign, seated on David's throne for 1,000 years. After He has done that, proving actual ownership of this planet, He will then present this deed of earth *back* to God, the Father. It will have come full circle.

Since Satan knows this *beyond doubt*, it is obvious that he wishes nothing more than to *stop* that from occurring. Barring his ability to stop the Rapture, he has created a *plausible* version of the event that his followers, along with the remaining people on earth, will *believe* (for the most part). Those who do not believe it will probably not last too long, and may well keep quiet, though they themselves may finally become saved because of it. If so, they will become one of those who evangelize the world, though it is clear from Revelation that the 144,000 who are sealed with God's seal will do the lion's share of that (cf. Revelation 7 and 14), and are *Jewish*. These Jewish believers will fulfill what has always been God's intention for the nation of Israel.

The Rapture? Oh Come *ON!*
When the Rapture *does* occur (see previous chapter), Satan will have already created an acceptable reason for the instantaneous absence of millions of people in *less* than a second. With the Church gone, "he who restrains" will also step aside (cf. 2 Thessalonians 2:7). The Holy

Spirit? Michael, the Archangel? If the Holy Spirit, He who worked through millions of Christians since the birth of the Church, will move *aside* and, for a time, there is no one left to work directly *through*. The gates of hell will begin to open and Satan will literally run rampant along with hordes of Nephilim spirits (demons) and fallen angels, doing what they set their minds to doing, all under the auspices of God's sovereignty. The preparations, which have been going on behind the scenes since the *fall of man,* and certainly since the death and resurrection of Jesus Christ, will finally come into *full* view. The New Age adherents will finally *see* their *messiah* and woe to them because of the great evil he conceals and brings.

While many Christians today waste time *quarreling* over the biblical veracity of events such as the Rapture and the Second Coming, this is not the case for those within the New Age. It seems that *most* within the New Age movement have no problem accepting a future event in which millions will disappear off the face of this planet in an *instant*. Satan has prepared their minds for this event, and it will not take them by surprise. Certainly, the event itself may *shock* them, due to its enormity and instantaneous nature, but as soon as they regain their composure, they will praise the name of their god because now – *finally* – the world and its citizens can *advance* to the next spiritual plane, with nothing blocking the way.

The modern New Age movement grew out of the hippie movement of the 1960s. Once the Beatles hit their stride, love, peace, and Transcendental Meditation became the staples of our society. People turned against *any* reason for war.

Involved in communal living, and a great deal of meditation, drugs, and yoga, these people seemed harmless enough, though deluded to the rest of the world. Unfortunately, they have become anything *but* harmless, having become channels through which Satan has worked his schemes to dominate the world. As the Christian longs for the reward of heaven and an eternity with Jesus, the New Ager longs for the final "Christ" revealing, in order to watch the ushering in of a new world order.

Early in this country's development, the *"Adventist movement founded by William Miller experienced 'great disappointments' of 1843 and 1844. That movement was based upon the premise that the 'Great Falling Away' or apostasy of Thessalonians had already occurred between the era of Constantine and the Reformation during a 1,260-year period. This 'apostasy' would reveal the 'Man of Perdition,' whom they believed to be the Catholic pope."*[1] This is one of the dangers, by the way, of allegorizing Scriptures, as evidenced here. These beliefs stem from a purely *spiritualized* view of the Bible. Nothing is viewed with a literal meaning with respect to Eschatology or prophecy.

Cumby explains that it was not merely the Adventist movement, which held this view, but other Protestant denominations believed this as well. At the same time though, many still believed that the Old Testament prophecies regarding Israel had not yet been fulfilled. It created a confused, allegorized understanding of prophetic discourse, which only seemed *loosely* based on the Bible. This of course, is Satan's work, part of his strategy to create a one-world religion.

Prophecy Goes Allegorical

The Adventists, who opted to interpret these prophecies in *spiritual* terms, rather than *literal* created not a few problems. *"Interpreting this prophecy to mean a 'spiritual Israel' rather than a political Israel, the Adventists felt that all prophecies were fulfilled except for the 'Great Commission' – the command to preach the gospel to all nations."*[47]

Of course, eventually history tells us that Israel *did* once again become a nation. This took place in 1948, and it has been variously interpreted to mean different things, depending upon the group.

---

[47] Constance Cumby, *The Hidden Dangers of the Rainbow* (Shreveport: Huntington House 1983), 36

Some view this as a complete *accident* of nature. Others believe that it *is* of God, as things moved toward fulfillment.

Ever since then, passions on all sides of the issue have erupted within the church, with people pointing fingers, calling each other names and in general, vilifying those with opposing positions regarding Israel and the potential prophetic nature of its restoration. To those *outside* the visible Church, this would simply serve to reinforce their view that hypocrites make up the Church. They further believe that the people in the Church have no truth, but certainly know how to fight with each other.

Cumby explains, "*What nearly every 'Christian' name-caller overlooked were the plain and simple biblical specifications of the spirit of antichrist and the fact that a Movement meeting these specifications was growing under their noses and even influencing their churches.*"[48]

The New Age has changed much over the last twenty to thirty years. We are now experiencing the last stage of a movement. This will culminate with the revelation of the one who Paul describes as "*that man of sin be revealed, the son of perdition; Who opposeth and exalteth himself above all that is called God, or that is worshipped; so that he as God sixtieth in the temple of God, showing himself that he is God,*" (2 Thessalonians 2:3b-4).

The End is Coming
It is interesting to consider that both Christians and New Agers are *waiting* for the culmination of this age. Both groups are waiting for their individual messiahs; the Church awaits the return of Jesus Christ and the New Age awaits the revelation of the Antichrist, thought to be the *real* Christ. Because of their consistent rejection of authentic salvation, preferring instead to rely on their own strength, power, and ability, they will get their wish to see if they can become *gods*.

---

[48] Constance Cumby, *The Hidden Dangers of the Rainbow* (Shreveport: Huntington House 1983), 37

Certainly, they will be encouraged to do so by the Antichrist himself. Bowing in worship to him will not seem one bit unusual. After all, he will be the *epitome* of what they wish to become and since to them, god is in everything and all is god, worshipping him is worshipping *themselves.*

Those who doubt the prophecies regarding the end times, are looking for no one, due to their belief that Christ's return was/is an event taking place within the spiritual realm, or has already taken place in A.D. 70. They will likely be shocked when the Rapture occurs and possibly, before that, a northern attempted invasion into Israel, which will be easily handled by God Himself.

Satan merely *appears* to have his bases covered. He has fooled all the groups that need fooling with the perfect lie for each; a lie that convinces each group that what *they* believe is the correct belief. His fallen angels and Nephilim demons have been working around the clock to achieve for their *master* the plan he created and has worked so hard to achieve. Of course, we know that ultimately, this plan has been carefully created yet *fully* overseen by God's' sovereignty.

Because of their work, the New Age movement has become a force that the world *will* reckon with and a force that is fast becoming a spiritual *powerhouse*, both outside and unfortunately, *inside* the visible Church. Ultimately, true Christians are aware of the fact that Satan moves *only* as God *allows.* His temporary kingdom stands and falls by God's *will.* The revelation of all false prophets and those claiming to be Maitreya along with everything else connected to Satan's plan through the New Age is under God's careful scrutiny and full sovereignty.

No Worries – God is Sovereign
In spite of what the New Age *has* become or *will* evolve into, God is absolutely in command. His throne has never, nor will ever be in jeopardy. The pretenders and wannabes, who seek to *unseat* Him in

order to *usurp* Him, will be shown for *who* and *what* they really are, along with the true power that motivates and empowers them. They, along with their evil mentor will one day, at the correct and predetermined time will come to a violent and quick end.

The only One standing will be the only true Ruler, God Himself, Jesus Christ, along with those who stand with Him. For that, we praise His Name and look for His coming.

Chapter 7
Speaking Words of Truth?

I place a curse on anyone who dares come against this ministry!!!*

PREACH IT!

Penny Winn Ministries

Modern Day "Prophets" *Curse Those Who Try to Thwart Their Ministry

*http://www.intotruth.org/wof/Hinn.html

©2010 F. DERUVO

It is ironic that in today's society, Christians are often labeled "intolerant" and "arrogant." This is because we apparently have the audacity to suggest, or even clearly teach, that there is only *one* way to gain salvation and that is *through* the Lord Jesus Christ.

His atonement on Calvary's cross that was purchased for humanity the opportunity to re-establish a relationship with God. We call this salvation, and if not for what Christ accomplished on the cross, that way back to God for salvation would forever remain closed with the failure of Adam and Eve, in Genesis 3.

Authentic Christians Believe What Christ Said

Christians are simply echoing what Jesus said about Himself in John 14:6, "*Jesus saith unto him, I am the way, the truth, and the life: no man cometh unto the Father, but by me.*" To everyone who is not a Christian, and sees no reason to become one, this statement is extremely *arrogant*. How can there be only one way, or one truth? Certainly, it cannot be argued that many have seen, and do see the truth, as being *relative*, morphing as the circumstances merit, into something plausible and, which meets the needs of that particular situation.

In one swell swoop though, not only did Christ negate this errant viewpoint, but He also knocked every other pretender to the throne right off the table. He was saying, clearly and directly, that there is only *one* salvation and salvation comes only *from* and *through* Him. It comes *from* no one else. Jesus instantly labeled every other messiah wannabe *false*.

Not long ago on my Blog, I had written about a particular religious group. Because of their origins *and* beliefs, they have come under fire for being cult-like. While some would not agree with my understanding of their beliefs as being a works-based salvation (an offshoot of Romanism), it seems clear enough to me (and many others), that their understanding of salvation makes them *wrong*, and because they *add* to salvation with works, in my mind, they are a cult. Their very religious sect is keeping people from finding the one, true salvation because they have muddied the waters, and covered authentic salvation with numerous works that must also be accomplished in order to actually *secure* salvation. I do not find this taught in Scripture.

While it is certainly possible that people within some of these sects can actually find their way to receiving authentic salvation, the belief system more often than not keeps people from getting to that point of understanding. It is very much like the Pharisees who emphasized *works*. They unfortunately made it so difficult to receive salvation, that they themselves did not have it, and their codes, laws, and interpretations of all of it kept the common person from receiving salvation as well.

Regarding my Blog, one individual commented how he thought I was being very *judgmental* and *irresponsible*. I responded that I did not believe I was being either of those things. My concern is that the people involved in that group (and he is one by his own admission) have *changed* salvation by adding to it. They need to be informed.

We went back and forth a few times, and I finally asked him if he would please tell me his definition of salvation. To that he responded with, "*I believe that I do not have all of the answers. I believe that everyone has the right to worship God in the way that feels right to them as long as they are not harming or persecuting others. Most of all I believe that different denominations & different religions are different paths to the same destination. May God Bless You.*"[49]

That man's answer is tragic. He has likely not found salvation. However, though I cannot be sure, I want *him* to be sure, don't you? Just prior to answering the question I posed about salvation, he made a comment about Mormons and Jehovah's Witnesses. He said, "*Although I may not personally hold all of the same beliefs as the Mormons or Jehovah's Witnesses, I believe that it is equally irresponsible and incorrect to label those denominations "cult-like" as well.*"[50]

It is clear that this poor man seems to have no clue *what* he believes. He cannot say distinctly what his particular beliefs are about salvation, and he simply sits back mouthing the words that I am being judgmental and irresponsible. Well if I *am* being that because I

---

[49] http://modres.wordpress.com/2009/12/29/seventh-day-adventism-trying-to-hide/#comments
[50] Ibid

want people to come to know Jesus Christ as Savior, then I will continue to be that.

Another individual, also following up on the Blog warned that Jesus has people of ALL faiths (her emphasis) as His children. She then accused me of throwing stones. The fallacy exists among people like this that God is a *sentimentalist*. They thrive on seeing a loving sentimentality that *they* believe saves people, because since God is *love* then He will not allow people of other faiths to die without salvation. Again, this is nothing more than rank sentimentality. I fully believe that God saves people *out of* all faiths, but to suggest that God saves them *within* those faiths, so that they do not need to *leave* those faiths, is another thing altogether. Yet, this is part of the New Age/Emergent Church dogma.

Oh, the Arrogance!

So the true Christian, because he teaches that salvation comes only through Jesus Christ, is labeled arrogant, irresponsible, or not in harmony with society. Authentic Christians are like viruses that, if left by themselves, will work their way through society, ruining it as they go. The Christian has no clue, people say as they roll their eyes, and smile knowingly to one another.

Does this Christian not realize that he is *offending* every other religion and/or culture by that statement? Does he not realize that he is *not* making friends with anyone, but creating enemies instead? Their smiles will eventually turn to anger and then hatred, as time marches on toward the end.

Who does the Christian *serve*? Are we really to be concerned about what the *world* teaches? Are we to fear rejection by the world because what we teach is so inclusive and separating? Our utmost concern should be for each person's spiritual welfare. Do they know Christ or not? Have they realized their *need* for salvation? If not, they have no salvation.

Granted, Christians can sometimes be overbearing about the way they attempt to evangelize. At one point in life, I used the "get in your face" approach. It does not work. A good method is what Kirk Cameron and Ray Comfort[51] teach. It works because it simply replicates what Jesus did when He walked this earth.

Jesus participated in relational *discipleship*. He did *not* do relational *evangelism*, where one takes time to get to know someone. Over the space of that time, they get to see how the Christian life is lived within the person. They hope that it may serve to open the door to communication and evangelization, yada, yada, yada. The difficulty is that we do not know when *we* will die, much less anyone else. Can we really take the time to use relational evangelism as our *prime* choice in our evangelistic efforts?

Jesus also did *not* get in people's faces with "you're going to hell if you do not repent" routine either. Yes, He spoke of hell (often), but He normally brought people around to comparing their lives with the Ten Commandments and once they did that, they often began to see for themselves that if God were to judge them based on *His* Law, they would fail, miserably, as we *all* would. From there, it is one additional step to helping them understand that Jesus came to pay the price for us. His salvation extends to all people, yet only those who believe in Him receive it.

At the roots of things though are the same forces of evil that have been working since *their* fall (and/or birth in the case of the Nephilim), not only to undermine the will of God but also His purposes. They wish to create their own morality and their own "salvation," which we know is no salvation at all. What the man just quoted *preached* to me on my Blog is nothing more than New Age propaganda, wrapped in religious clothing. It is like a wolf in sheep's clothing. It *sounds* kind of good, but underneath is death.

---

[51] http://wayofthemaster.com/

Leaders Going Blind

Frankly, I believe that the fallen angels *and* the Nephilim demons have been working to perpetrate a massive delusion, which sounds and seems reasonable to the average individual. Individuals who appear to be *ministers* of Christ, unfortunately, often carry on the work of this fallen spiritual underworld.

The religious leaders who stand in the pulpit week after week, have either lost their own vision (if they had one) for what God is doing in the world, or they have only cared about hearing the world's applause and accolades from the beginning. That temptation comes with the territory for *large* churches. It becomes a matter of financial *survival*, rather than continued *expositional* preaching the Word of God, in spite of what some may think of it, or how they react to it.

Think about some of these *mega*-churches and how much money it costs to run them weekly; salaries, supplies, utilities – all of it! Can pastors really take the chance of *offending* someone by preaching about *sin*, or breaking the Law of God, and our need for Him in salvation? If they did, there is a very real chance that they would drive at least some of the money-givers out of that church and into another. Loss of funds means loss of programs and salaries. Sad.

Actually, in today's modern world, it does not even have to be about salvation (though it often is). Each time the true Christian espouses an opinion that is *biblically*-based, and due to that, is seen as being against the current "norm" of society, then that same Christian becomes tagged with the *intolerant* or *judgmental* label.

Who would argue that the *reason* for which Jesus came was for salvation? Everything in His life led to that. He lived a life of sinless perfection, which qualified Him to be the sin offering in order that man might taste the goodness of God, found only in His salvation. It was for this purpose that He became a Man, while remaining *fully* God. We are told that He cried for Jerusalem because of their unbelief in Him, and their unwillingness to come to Him (cf. Luke 19: 41-44). Paul tells us that we (Gentiles) are *blessed* because of their (Jewish) unbelief (cf. Romans 11:11-24). It is important that we understand this because it is here that we realize the importance of God's salvation, in the form of preaching it, teaching it and living it.

Salvation is what Jesus came to accomplish. His death on the cross of Calvary provided that possibility for humanity. His salvation is *now* available. Is He being truthful when He says that He is the *way*, the *truth* and the *life*? Is He exaggerating His importance by essentially implying that salvation comes from no other individual? Not at all.

The New Age's Religious Garb

The road leading to eternal life is what Jesus referred to as the narrow path (cf. Matthew 7:14). He included the words "*and few be they that find it.*" Jesus was closing *every* other door. He was sealing up every other avenue that *claimed* to achieve or obtain salvation for anyone. Nothing outside of Jesus Himself enables a person to arrive at the proper gate. We enter in *only* through Him.

Salvation is certainly the most important issue *every* individual faces. How each person responds to that issue is literally the difference be-tween eternal *life* and eternal *death*. The wrong response *here* will mean death in the afterlife *there*.

Nevertheless, today, many clearly teach *another* gospel, or way of salvation. Many suggest or go so far as to state that salvation *is* found elsewhere, *other* than Christ. This has been the norm within the New Age movement and most of us are aware of it, but what about the visible Church itself? What is going on there?

There are a number of "big" names in the field of religion. Many of those names are also associated with what we know as the Emergent Church; something that is really nothing more than the New Age in religious garb. The Emergent Church has brought the realm of *mysticism* into the visible Church with the emphasis in these churches based on *feeling* (in contrast to gaining a better understanding of God's Word). It is in *experiencing* God that people get to know Him better (we are told by leaders within the Emergent Church). There are often more questions *asked* than answered as well within those churches that have adopted the Emergent approach. The idea is that there may not actually be *one* right answer, so it is better to simply ask questions, bounce ideas around, and come to a consensus. The Bible is often pushed off to the side, and it is used as a last resort in many cases. None of this is too different from what the New Age (or space aliens!) teach.

How You Doin' J-Man?!

The tone of an Emergent Church is casual. People dress casually (including the person who oversees the service). The pulpit is normally set aside, often replaced by a music stand and possibly even a stool or chair used by the "Overseer" or "host" if you will. From there, a message is presented that normally includes funny jokes, an upbeat delivery, and a verse or two of Scripture here and there. One easily gets the impression that if Jesus actually appeared in one of these services, the people might think that they could walk right up to Him and shout, *"Yo, J-Man. What up!?"* with a slap on the back. It seems that what Peter, James and John did as a reaction to the Transfiguration (cf. Matthew 17:1-9, Mark 9:2-8, Luke 9:28-36) is the furthest thing from anyone's mind in many of today's churches.

Preaching in these churches is not really preaching as much as it is giving a *message*. The message is usually topical, how to have *friends*, how to *break free*, how to do this or that. These types of messages emphasize how people can *use* God to get to the next level, whatever that may be. Of course, this varies from person to person.

Rock On!

Normally, the music is bright, even rocky, or what some might term *worldly*. The entire demeanor of these "worship" services caters to people who are "seeker sensitive." In other words, these churches are trying to reach out to people who do not yet know Christ. This is certainly good, but unfortunately, not only do they wind up not teaching them anything about salvation, but the individuals who attend who might already be saved are not fed any meat, but merely milk.

Please don't misunderstand the point. I have played drums for years, and I do not mind upbeat music. However, it had better be *uplifting* and *honoring to God* as well. The trouble is that much of today's so-called Christian music is that in *name* only. There is very little if any Christian theology built into many of these songs. The hymns of old, which have a good deal of Scriptural depth to them, have been replaced with *feel-good* choruses, that have a beat and you can dance to them.

Worship should be just that; *worship* and that is difficult to do if the words only include feel-good phrases, with music that is much the same. The music and singing should instill a deep sense of *reverence*, *humility*, *love,* and *awe* for God. It should *not* make you want to dance and jiggle.

Many leaders today within the Emergent Church have actually come out and suggested that maybe Jesus is *not* the only way, or to be more exact, they may say that *Christianity* is not necessarily the *only* way (though Jesus is), as Tony Campolo has stated in numerous ways:

"I am saying that there is no salvation apart from Jesus; that's my evangelical mindset. However, I am not convinced that Jesus only lives in Christians."

"...what can I say to an Islamic brother who has fed the hungry, and clothed the naked? You say, 'But he hasn't a personal relationship with Christ.' I would argue with that. And I would say from a Christian perspective, in as much as you did it to the least of these you did it unto

Christ. You did have a personal relationship with Christ, you just didn't know it."

The above two comments are from Tony Campolo and he is one of those in the forefront of the Emergent Church movement. His comments do not even need to be considered closely to understand that he beliefs and espouse heresy. He is saying that Jesus lives in *others* who are not necessarily Christians, and even within people who are *not* aware of His presence. Yet, this appears to be in direct *opposition* to what Jesus Himself said. Campolo's gospel is *another* gospel. Though it *feels* good, it offers *nothing* but death in the end.

The fact that Mr. Campolo believes that Jesus *can* live in others who are not Christians means that *he* believes there is a salvation that others can experience *apart* from Christ and Christianity. They might be Muslim (as his second comment indicates), or within those who are members of cults, or something else entirely.

He bases this opinion on the fact that these people *may* have led socially *valuable* or *good* lives, in that they spent time feeding the hungry and clothing the naked. The truth of the particular parable – the Sheep and the Goats, as Campolo alludes to – is best understood (like all truth of Scripture) within its *context*, found in Matthew 25:31–46. There are generally two interpretations of this particular parable. One way to view this is as one of the last judgments of Christ after His return to earth, when He sets up His earthly kingdom, after the end of the Great Tribulation.

Christ will judge those nations based on how they took care of the Jews who had just gone through tremendously evil persecution led by Antichrist. While His basis *seems* to be judging them on what they *did*, the reality is that only those who were Christian *during* the Tribulation/Great Tribulation would have had the proper outlook enough to even *want* to help Jews since to do so and be caught will likely mean the same retributive response by Antichrist. Most people, no matter how moral they believe themselves to be, will *not* go out of their way to help someone, if it means that the action of helping someone else will put their own life in jeopardy.

I was watching one of those "the dumbest things people do" shows the other night. In one segment, it showed a unique race. People start at the top of a sandy hill, with spectators lining each side and at the bottom, enjoying the race from their vantage points.

Actually, it was not so much a race, as it was individuals riding weird, homemade creations down the hill. The object seemed to be to arrive at the bottom without getting hurt. Everything went fairly well, until three individuals came up for their turn. They had taken a living room sofa, attached wheels to the bottom of it, and were going to ride it down the large hill, which had a steep slant to it.

As they began their descent, the sofa picked up speed, going faster and faster. Unfortunately, their design for the sofa did *not* include a way to *stop* or *steer* it. It went wherever the wheels took it.

There were people on both sides of the lane, starting about halfway down toward the finish. On the right side looking up at the hill, a number of small groups of people sat, enjoying the event. What happened next happened quickly. A group of three people sitting too close to the edge of the action realized that the sofa had veered toward them.

There was a man closest to the lane, who saw what was happening, and jumped over the two girls who were part of his group. He managed to jump out of the way of the hurtling sofa, but the one edge of it slammed into one of the girls. The sofa flipped end over end, ejecting its occupants in all directions. They did somersaults in the air, eventually landing at the finish line, which had been buttressed by mattresses and things of that nature. Immediately behind them, the sofa crashed *onto* them.

Of course, there were injuries, as people just lay there motionless. Spectators scrambled to help any way they could. The man who had jumped out of the way would have received the brunt of the sofa's brute force. However, note that as he jumped out of the way, he jumped *over* the two girls. His (and our) natural response is to either fight or flee. He chose to flee and saved himself from injury, but he was *not* thinking about saving anyone else. In truth, there was likely just enough time for him to *react*, not think about anyone else that he might be able to save.

Thinking of Number One

So the point is that though this man who jumped out of the way might have thought himself to be a very moral person, he actually thought *only* of himself and *his* survival when push came to shove. This is true with *all* people. Even Christians have to be taught to think of others first, because it is not necessarily automatic.

Those judged by Christ in the Sheep and the Goats Judgment are judged based on their works. However, these works are a natural *outflow* of their inner man. This is what some people did for Jewish individuals during the rise of the Third Reich. Corrie Ten Boom is noted for her willingness to hide Jews from the Nazis during that period. Because of her actions (and others like her), many Jews were saved from Hitler's death camps. Why did they do this? They did what they did because of their own salvation in Christ Jesus.

The other way of viewing this parable of the Sheep and the Goats is to see *all* the individuals as Christians, some who have little or nothing and others who have more. How did those Christians who had more relate to those who had little? In other words, was their faith real so that as James would say, their faith was seen in their action (James 2:18)? Unfortunately, this is a *works-based salvation*, and though often taught like this in numerous Emergent Churches, it fully misrepresents Jesus, James, Paul, and other NT writers.

One Step Forward; Two Steps Back

As Dr. MacArthur relates in his book *Why One Way?*, society has gone beyond Modernism, having entered into what is termed Postmodernism. "*Postmodernists have repudiated modernism's absolute confidence in science as the only pathway to the truth. In fact, postmodernism has completely lost interest in 'the truth' insisting that there is no thing as absolute, objective, or universal truth.*"[52]

So what was once considered truth has now been replaced by something that leaves truth completely up for grabs. In that sense, truth has become *relative*, ultimately decided by the individual himself. Subjectivism's view of truth is no different from what existed during Pilate's day, when truth was up for grabs then as well. Because of the proliferation of the Greek and Roman gods and goddesses, different people, depending upon their own particular view of a god or gods they worshipped, saw truth differently. Our society is fast becoming exactly like this, if we are not there already.

Since truth is seen as *changing*, with each person subjectively deciding upon its relevance, it is no wonder then that the Christian's "one way" view of salvation is not only seen as antiquated and unenlightened, but as a real problem for those who believe truth is too large to be relegated to *one* thing. This view is fast becoming the norm throughout society.

We Are All Gods

Not long ago, during a special taping of a daytime talk show, a well-known host had as her guest, another well-known author, within the New Age arena. Because of a number of books he had written, he literally had become a household name (with the host's help). His books speak of a god in which *all* participate. In fact, his main message is similar to the messages presented by countless New Age adherents; *we are gods*. We simply fail to realize our full potential.

---

[52] John MacArthur, *Why One Way?* (W. Publishing Group 2002), 7

Once we appreciate our full potential, we *unlock* our own deity within, and the last phase of our salvation will begin.

The interesting thing of course is that within many of these messages, Christian-sounding terms are used, mainly because of their familiarity. Rather than be off-putting to someone, words like *salvation* or similar terms tend to draw people in because they are already well known to most. They are merely given a different meaning, which turns out to be much more *inclusive.*

During the course of the show, a question and answer period was provided and one woman stood essentially stating that salvation came *only* from Jesus Christ and she quoted John 14:6. A number of audience members agreed with her and showed their agreement with applause. The nonplussed host simply shook her head and replied, *"There couldn't possibly be only one way. There couldn't possibly be."*

That is the way things are going these days and we can expect more of the same as time moves forward, coming closer to the end. It leads to the question of whether or not there *is* absolute truth. If there is, then Jesus has a strong argument in His favor. If there is no such thing as absolute truth, then His words of John 14:6 can be *ignored*, as coming from someone who really had no clue.

The Activity Behind the New Age Mask
Anyone who has studied the New Age knows all of this already, but the fact of the matter remains that if we could see *behind the spiritual veil*, which separates our world from the spiritual, we would see tremendous activity occurring all the time. Fallen angels and Nephilim demons, all answering to Satan, run back and forth to accomplish his ends.

The amount of energy and activity that constantly goes into bringing Satan's purposes to fruition must be astounding to see. Is it any wonder Peter warned us about the fact that Satan roams the earth seeking someone whom he can devour, and Paul tells us to pray without ceasing? (cf. 1 Peter 5:8; 1 Thessalonians 5:17)

For most people today, truth is merely one variable. It is common to hear comments designed to tell people that a particular truth is fine for *them*, but others may need a *different* truth. So begins a long line of subjectivity of truth that looks different to each person.

Why do we do this? The largest reason likely has to do with what Dr. MacArthur states in his book *The Truth War.* We attempt to be friends with the world. We want to be seen in a favorable light, so we do not want to take the chance of doing things that may ruffle feathers, or offend someone outright.

Yet, this is *not* what Jesus did. He often publicly rebutted and rebuked the religious leaders of His time. These leaders ensnared people by *hiding* the truth of the gospel under layers of rabbinical teaching and oral tradition. This hidden truth was extremely difficult for the religious leaders to find and next to impossible for the average, common person, who relied on the teachings of the Scribes and Pharisees, to understand.

"Authentic Christianity has always held that Scripture is absolute, objective truth. It is as true for one person as it is for another, regardless of anyone's opinion about it. It has one true meaning that applies to everyone. It is God's Word to humanity, and its true meaning is determined by God; it is not something that can be shaped to fit the preferences of individual hearers."[53]

Unfortunately, this is less and less believed today even within the visible Church today. Is His Word objective truth or not? If not, then one moral rule or law is just as good as another is, provided the *majority* agrees with it. If it is objective, then to circumvent it by

---

[53] John MacArthur, *Why One Way?* (W. Publishing Group 2002), 26

trying to create something else entirely is to ignore God and His truth, and do exactly what Satan has been attempting to do for centuries. Every time Satan speaks, he lies as a matter of course. He will continue to lie in order to establish himself on God's throne. Because everything about him involves a lie, then his kingdom will not stand and has already been defeated at the cross.

In a day and age where truth is once again becoming tragically relative, authentic Christians stand out like proverbial sore thumbs. We only have two choices: 1) to attempt to *befriend* the world, or 2) to remain *steadfast* with God. It is *impossible* to do both.

Telling It Like It Is

James deals with the problem directly, teaching his readers that to have any type of friendship with the world, places us *against* God. He is not speaking of our associations with those in the world who are lost. He is speaking of having the *desires* of those who are lost. These people want things like money, fast and expensive cars, big homes, and lots of food, expensive vacations, and much more. They really do not care who they step on to acquire those things. James is not arguing that people are not allowed to work hard enough to buy a car, or have enough food for their family, or want to own their own home. James is, instead *insisting* that those who have these desires *solely* and *primarily* wind up placing themselves in *opposition* to God, *enslaving* themselves to those desires.

James clearly brings this out in his epistle, "*From whence come wars and fightings among you? come they not hence, even of your lusts that war in your members? Ye lust, and have not: ye kill, and desire to have, and cannot obtain: ye fight and war, yet ye have not, because ye ask not. Ye ask, and receive not, because ye ask amiss, that ye may consume it upon your lusts. Ye adulterers and adulteresses, know ye not that the friendship of the world is enmity with God? whosoever therefore will be a friend of the world is the enemy of God. Do ye think that the scripture saith in vain, The spirit that dwelleth in us lusteth to envy? But he giveth more grace. Wherefore he saith, God resisteth the proud, but giveth grace unto the humble. Submit yourselves therefore to God. Resist the devil, and he will flee from you. Draw nigh to God, and he will draw nigh to you. Cleanse your hands, ye sinners; and purify your hearts, ye double minded. Be afflicted, and mourn, and weep: let your laughter be turned to mourning, and your joy to heaviness. Humble yourselves in the sight of the Lord, and he shall lift you up,"* (James 4:1-10).

Friends to the World

Any Christian who seeks to be friends with world is making a terribly grave mistake. We are *not* here to befriend the world (cf. 1 John 2:15). We are here to preach the gospel by the *example* of our lives and the *words* of our mouth (James 1:22). It is impossible to do this while yearning for what the world has to offer. Yet too many Christians today are trying to do just that.

Christians need to take some time to read Foxe's Book of Martyrs. It would do us all good. These people stood for God against the very real and tremendous persecution of their day, yet they gave *no* ground. Instead, they preferred to die if necessary than wind up betraying the One who had given His life so that they might have salvation.

We are called *out* of the world, yet we are still living *in* the world. In that case, God obviously does not want us to sequester ourselves, trying to make ourselves an island. He wants to work *in* and *through* us as He calls people to Himself, until the fullness of the Gentiles has been established.

Chapter 8

It's All in the Theatrics

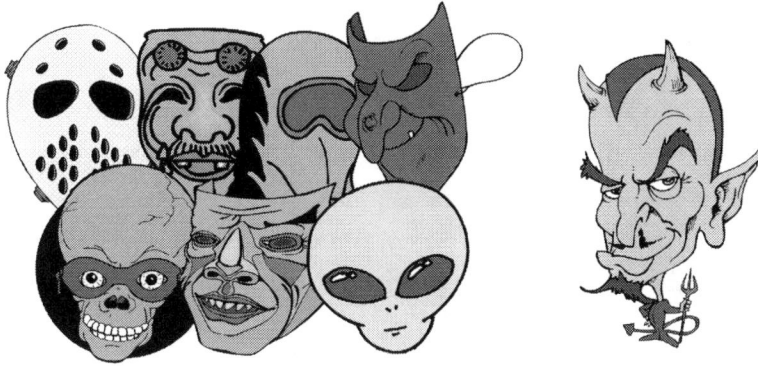

PEAK-A-BOO, HE SEES YOU!

"And as it was in the days of Noe, so shall it be also in the days of the Son of man." *(Luke 17:26)*

We have seen how Satan uses many things to bring about his chosen purposes. We know that he is architect of the New Age movement. We know that he has created a myriad of ideals and goals, designed to entangle many. We also know that his angels and the Nephilim demons do a lion's share of his bidding. Through them, intricate and complex systems are built on lies. Tarot Cards, the Ouija Board, Reiki, Transcendental Meditation, Breath Prayers/Contemplative Prayer, the use of Labyrinths, mixing aspects of other faiths and sects with Christianity, or any number of things serve to pull us from God and toward Satan. The reality is that Satan will stop at nothing to capture the hearts and imaginations of people throughout the world. We know that he has been doing that since Adam and Eve and since he requires no sleep, he works at it all the time, non-stop.

Perfecting the Ruse

Satan has had at least 4,000 years to perfect his techniques. He likely tried numerous things to destroy humankind, because of the way he understood God's Word (in the Garden of Eden). He got our first parents to sin, and with their sin, gained access to God's Creation as ruler of the air. When he realized that his efforts had not panned out the way he wanted them to (God implied that a Savior would be sent in Genesis 3), he got started on his plan to corrupt all of humanity.

At each step of the way, God was far ahead of Satan. God obviously kept for Himself Noah and his family. Since we know that *"Noah was a just man and perfect in his generations, and Noah walked with God,"* (Genesis 6:9b), then we gain a clue into the possibility that he was perfect in all his generations due to the fact that Satan had not been able to corrupt the Noahic line.

Chuck Missler points this out in his book *Alien Encounters*. It makes sense too. Since Satan had been *unable* to corrupt Noah's DNA, then the Messiah *could still be born* into humanity. If all of God's human creation became corrupted, then this could not have happened.

Luke is the only gospel in the New Testament in which Jesus makes the statement shown above. In the seventeenth chapter of Luke, Jesus is teaching and speaks of a number of things prior to making the noted statement regarding Noah. In His teaching, Jesus discusses things like increased faith, and the inevitability of sin, but "woe" to the one through whom sin is introduced to others. He also takes the time during His journey to Jerusalem to stop and heal ten lepers.

Those Annoying Pharisees

As usual, the Pharisees were not far behind Jesus, always looking for an opportunity to fault Him and find ways to condemn Him. Incidentally, orthodox Jewish men followed Paul from town to town in an attempt to turn people against him – cf. the book of Acts. This seems to be one of Satan's favorite strategies.

Satan and his minions used the Pharisees and religious leaders of Christ's day quite well. In this particular instance, the Pharisees asked Him a question regarding *when* God's Kingdom would arrive. Jesus answers simply by stating, "*And when he was demanded of the Pharisees, when the kingdom of God should come, he answered them and said, The kingdom of God cometh not with observation,*" (Luke 17:20).

Though He seemed on one hand to be denying a *physical* return (as some teach), it is apparent that Jesus was speaking of a kingdom that was *based in*, and started *with*, a spiritual *renewal*, something which was ultimately and *only* found in Jesus and His kingdom. At the same time though, He was not in any way negating the truth of His future, personal return (as proven in the verses immediately following, and also the first chapter of the book of Acts), since these two concepts are not mutually exclusive.

In truth, when Jesus said that the kingdom of God was in the midst of the Pharisees, He was obviously speaking of *Himself*, because He was standing right there among them. They could see Him. There was no fanfare. He was just there, and from all outward appearances, He did not appear to be anything other than a Jewish man.

Jesus continues with His teaching about the future arrival of His kingdom, comparing the circumstances surrounding its arrival with the time of Noah (as well as Sodom and Gomorrah). This is very important for us to grasp. Luke 17:26 He says, "*Just as it was in the days of Noah, so will it be in the days of the Son of Man. They were eating and drinking and marrying and being given in marriage, until the day when Noah entered the ark, and the flood came and destroyed them all.*" Here Jesus clearly states that the circumstances connected to His physical return will be very *similar* to that of Noah's day.

Likewise, beginning in verse 28, Jesus compares His future physical return to the time of *Lot*, when Sodom and Gomorrah were physically and literally destroyed. The circumstances surrounding the destruction first of the whole world with the global flood and then using fire and brimstone with Sodom and Gomorrah are intriguing. Jesus specifically chose these two situations as comparatives.

At least part of the reason He chose these two was due to the exclusiveness of the judgment that God sent in each case. In each case, many lives were lost. Beyond this, livestock was lost, homes destroyed, and *nothing* remained after each of these judgments poured out from God's hand, except destruction.

Both of these events described by Jesus *physically* occurred, as will His return. Just as the floodwaters carried everyone outside the Ark to their deaths, Jesus' own return will take everyone not watching and waiting by surprise, with immediate judgment following.

Just as the annihilation literally raining down upon the twin cities of Sodom and Gomorrah took everyone by surprise, so will Jesus' return affect the world the same way. The only individuals who were spared were Lot, his wife and their daughters. However, even *they* did not get much warning at all. In effect, the destruction of those twin cities took everyone by surprise.

Scoffing at the Truth
We are increasingly seeing this type of reaction to the preaching of Christ's Second Coming today, with much more regularity. People are more often quick to disagree with the idea that the world will see Jesus return *physically*. Many within Christendom prefer to think of

His return in *spiritual* terms, because a literal physical return simply sounds too fantastic and unbelievable to the average person. Jesus is actually going to come back to earth and set up His kingdom. This is difficult for most to picture.

This entire subject – part of the overarching prophetic discourse, which Scripture provides related to the end of the age – has become something that people downplay, deny, or ignore altogether. From a biblical viewpoint, it makes sense that this would be the attitude of many. It should be noted as well that it has only been within the last few decades that the denial of the physical return of Jesus has come to the fore within Christian circles.

Here are Jesus' words regarding Noah's world, *"They did eat, they drank, they married wives, they were given in marriage, until the day that Noah entered into the ark, and the flood came, and destroyed them all,"* (Luke 17:28). What He is obviously saying is that things were going on *normally*, at least as normally as can be expected in spite of the fact that people were extremely evil and perverted. Even *then*, people still did the normal, everyday things that most people do in their lives on a daily basis today. People ate and drank, were married, gave their children away in marriage, they bought and sold goods and planted crops and built buildings. These are all very normal things for people to do and it does not matter whether they are labeled evil or good by others. Evil is as evil does and the evil that existed then could have only existed due to much more than simply man's depravity.

The Nephilim

We have already discussed the origins of the Nephilim. Not only did they appear in Genesis 6, but also they apparently reared their ugly heads again, this time in Numbers 13 and 14. There, we read that out of the 12 spies who went in and came out of Canaan, ten of the twelve spies reported a completely *negative* situation, emphasizing no faith in God whatsoever. Only Joshua and Caleb, the two remaining spies, believed God *would* give them the victory and encouraged the people to go in and take what God had already given to them. It was simply a matter of physically taking it and that required faith in God's Word.

Many years later, David dealt with one of these individuals who quite possibly was a Nephilim himself; *Goliath*. This Philistine warrior, as it turns out, was the smallest of his four brothers (cf. 1 Samuel 17)! The Philistines were to have been destroyed by the invading Israelites when Joshua led eventually led them into the land after their forty-year wilderness walk. Unfortunately, they failed to obey God here. Because of that, the Philistines became a thorn in the side of Israel and remained such for many generations.

Does this have anything at all to do with society today? It sounds far-fetched to be speaking of angels somehow entering into physical relations with human women. It also sounds far-fetched to talk of offspring, which are essentially *hybrids* of this union. The Nephilim that resulted from such a union are described as *giants*.

Because of the alleged abilities of these Nephilim, is it so difficult to imagine that in the realm where they exist *now* (the spirit world), their powers go beyond our ability to comprehend? Could these Nephilim, along with Satan and his workers of iniquity have the ability to manipulate the reality that *we* currently live in?

Not only do I think it is possible, but I believe that this is *exactly* what is happening and has been happening for generations. Jacques Vallee concluded that far from being actual space aliens, these beings that seem to travel in and out of our dimension at will, are just that – *inter*-dimensional beings, as opposed to interplanetary.

Are there any hints in Scripture at all that lend any credibility to this concept? There are a number of them.

Chapter 9

The Power of the Dark Side

The thing that I find absolutely intriguing, has to do with something we may not consider seriously. In Jacques Vallee's book called *Confrontations*, he details numerous cases of alien *interference* in the lives of individuals all over the world. He points out a number of situations, which have resulted in physical harm or *death* for some who have gotten in the path of either aliens or their crafts.

Vallee's Findings

Vallee referenced individuals who were shot at with some type of high-powered light beam. In some cases, the beam made noise and in others, it did not. However, in *all* cases, the result was either immediately fatal to the unfortunate human, the person died from complications later, or became injured in some way, from which they never fully recovered.

Alien Death Ray

At least one individual was seen to literally *evaporate* inside a beam of light, by his 14-year-old son. No trace of him was left behind. He was gone just like that. One cannot help but wonder whether things like this happen because the aliens wish to present events that will be remembered when the Rapture takes place.

Also interesting is the fact that some individuals who encountered an alien craft, found that injuries they *did* have for a good portion of their lives were now *gone*. After reading through Vallee's book, it is impossible to come to any conclusion other than the fact that these beings are *unpredictable* at best. They hold to no discernable pattern. In my mind, it appears as though they simply toy with us.

The fact that they *have* harmed people says a great deal. The fact that they have "healed" individuals also says something, but it may in fact say the same thing. In other words, these beings are very *powerful* beings. They have the ability to *manipulate*, whether physically, or non-physically. They can cause harm, and they can *appear* to heal.

Numerous sightings related in Vallee's book describe trees bent over to the breaking point (yet not always breaking), accomplished with the complete *absence* of *wind*. On other occasions, ships would touch down and after liftoff, leave behind a residue and an indentation on the ground.

This residue caused the growth rate of plants and weeds to increase in the vicinity. In at least one case, weeds that had a normal height of 3 feet grew to over 8 feet tall.

Testing the residue proved that it contained minerals and chemicals all of which are natural to various places on earth. However, the interesting thing is that a number of these minerals are never found together, nor are they found in some of the areas where they were left behind by these space ships.

Vallee speaks of many situations seen by other individuals; a number of them never spoke to authorities or anyone else about the events. They did open up to Vallee and he was surprised to find a mixed bag of ingredients in each situation. Though many of the events had similarities, no two events were alike.

Throughout researching many of these events and speaking with a myriad of people, Vallee concluded that these beings are *not* interplanetary beings at all. He believes that they are *inter-dimensional* beings, able to go from their own dimension to ours and out again very quickly, with no difficulty, because their dimension must butt right up against ours.

Lynne Dickie, interviewed in L. A. Marzulli's book (*The Alien Interviews)* notes that while she was under (what she now understands to be demonic influence), these beings would show her things in the sky. She saw a multitude of wormholes that made her think of an extremely busy ant farm. The beings indicated that they used these wormholes to gain access to and from earth.

If this is the case, it is something that we are obviously unable to do, because we are human, and lack the technology, in spite of what many Sci-Fi shows would have us believe. Vallee also seems to believe that these beings have the power to cause the human beings they encounter or "abduct," to fully believe that what they are experiencing is *real*, though may not actually be happening in our physical world, as in the case of the people stating that they have had out of body experiences caused by aliens. Did they really have an out of body experience, or a very strong illusion of it?

Even though there does not seem to be a great deal of information in the Bible, we do gain some insight into these beings and of what they are capable. We can refer to Jesus *after* His resurrection to see if there is anything different between His ability *before* and *after.*

Walking Through Walls

Of course, we need to be careful here, because it might be difficult to impossible arriving at solid conclusions based on the experiences of Jesus *after* His resurrection. What He did may be due to the fact that He is God. Nonetheless, looking at the example of His life, as well as other events throughout Scripture may shed some light on this subject for us.

In the case of Christ, if we consider the fact that He was able to walk *through* walls after His resurrection, this may tell us that in *our* glorified bodies, physical objects will prove to be no barrier against us. We also know that He made a *fire*, *caught* fish, and *cooked* it over that fire while waiting for some of the disciples. Does this tell us anything?

In the Gospel of John 21, we read the narrative of Jesus after His resurrection. Here He is on the beach in the early morning to meet His disciples who had been fishing. As they approached the shore, Jesus asked them in verse 5, "*Then Jesus saith unto them, Children, have ye any meat? They answered him, No.*" Jesus then said if they cast their nets on the right side of the ship, they would catch fish. In fact, the catch was so large that the net was too heavy to pull into the boat!

Following this, he cooked fish and with bread, gave it to the disciples. There is nothing in the text that states that Jesus *ate* with the disciples, but there is nothing that says He did *not.* However, the fact remains that Jesus' body was a type of *physical* body. He walked on the ground, was able to touch objects, He spoke, and was understood by His disciples. Beyond this, he took up physical *space*. He was *not* an apparition.

In Luke 24, we read of a number of things that Jesus did, which surprise us because of His ability to both relate *to the physical*, yet not be *bound by the physical*. This section of Scripture is the famous Emmaus road event, in which Jesus is walking and catches up with two of His disciples (one of which was Cleopas), who were discussing the recent events surrounding and including Jesus' death.

The Greatest Teacher of All!

As they walked, Jesus asked them why they were sad. They filled Him in on the events that had taken place and why they felt as though everything had come to an abrupt end. Jesus responded by saying, "*Then he said unto them, O fools, and slow of heart to believe all that the prophets have spoken: Ought not Christ to have suffered these things, and to enter into his glory? And beginning at Moses and all the prophets, he expounded unto them in all the scriptures the things concerning himself,*" (Luke 24:25-27).

From there, they ended up in the village and though Jesus appeared as if He was going to continue walking on, they insisted that He remain with them, since it was almost evening. He did so and they ate together. During the meal, He took bread and blessed it, broke it, and gave it to them. This would have instantly reminded them of the last supper with Him.

The text then states, "*And their eyes were opened, and they knew him; and he vanished out of their sight,*" (Luke 24:31). Jesus just went "poof" and was gone from out of their sight. Did He really disappear, or did He merely step out of *our* dimension and completely into the spiritual realm? The latter is likely what happened. To the disciples left at the table, they were astonished (and who would *not* be?) and remembered that as they walked with Jesus and listened to Him expound the Scriptures, their hearts "burned" within them.

We know throughout the Gospels that Jesus continually did things that confound us because they *seem* to ignore our scientific laws. He healed people. He raised the dead. He fed 5,000 and then 10,000. He recreated a man's two blind eyes, which is fascinating in and of itself, with the way Jesus did that miracle.

The text states, "*And he cometh to Bethsaida; and they bring a blind man unto him, and besought him to touch him. And he took the blind man by the hand, and led him out of the town; and when he had spit on his eyes, and put his hands upon him, he asked him if he saw ought. And he looked up, and said, I see men as trees, walking. After that he put his hands again upon his eyes, and made him look up: and he was restored, and saw every man clearly,*" (Mark 8:22-25). This account is so interesting. Though Christ could have healed the man's eyes perfectly with merely a thought, it appears as though He actually took the time to *recreate* the man's eyes, by forming *new* ones from mud, created from dirt and His spit. During the process, one can only imagine what the blind man might have been thinking. Imagine, someone reaching into the dirt, spitting on it, mixing it together (and you can see none of this, but possibly only hear Him spit), then *applies* that mud to your eyes. This takes faith to remain there and not run away thinking that the individual who is supposed to heal your eyes is a *lunatic*!

At first, the man could only see people as if they were *trees*. Jesus makes an "adjustment" by placing His hands over the man's eyes a second time, and then the man was able to see perfectly. Again, Christ could have done this from a distance, with merely a thought, but chose to do it this way for any number of reasons. This act of "creation" certainly proved His deity once again, but it also allowed the man to *exercise* his faith. The man's faith did *not* provide the healing. The man's faith *established* a confidence in the Creator and gave that faith a chance to grow *because* the healing was not instantaneous.

Jesus did many miracles *prior* to His physical death. Yet, in at least some cases, others participated in them. We know of the Transfiguration (cf. Matthew 17:1-9, Mark 9:2-8, Luke 9:28-36), where the physical veil of Jesus' body was temporarily set aside, allowing His glory *and* glorified body to show through. We also know that Peter, James, and John were there and witnessed the event.

In another situation, Jesus walked on water. We read that the seas were stormy. *"But the ship was now in the midst of the sea, tossed with waves: for the wind was contrary. And in the fourth watch of the night Jesus went unto them, walking on the sea,"* (cf. Matthew 14:24-25). Of course, they are upset, thinking they see some type of phantom, or ghost, but Jesus quickly calms them. You cannot blame the disciples. After all, if we were in the same situation, it would likely cause us to panic as well. It is not bad enough that the seas are tossing around as they are, but now there is a ghost walking toward them on the water seemingly undisturbed by the fury of the waves and wind!

Once they learned that it was Jesus and not some unknown phantom, Peter still wants to be sure, so he says that if it is really Jesus, He should call him (Peter) to walk out onto the sea with Him. Without hesitation, Jesus does so and Peter lifts one leg over the side of the boat followed by the other. Before he realizes it, he is actually walking on the water! We know how it ends. Peter begins to look around and starts to sink. We have to give credit to Peter though. How many of us would have dared to do what Peter did?

The point is that if Jesus allowed and even encouraged Peter to walk on water, maybe this act was not necessarily relegated to *divinity*. Maybe it is how we will actually interact with the natural elements in eternity future, and how Adam and Eve *did* interact with nature prior to the fall. Yes, this is merely an educated guess and in no way should be taken to mean that this author is dogmatic about it.

Did Adam Also Have the Ability?

However, what *is* interesting is found in the command God gave to Adam, that he should *"have dominion over the fish of the sea, and over the fowl of the air, and over every living thing that moveth upon the earth,"* (Genesis 1:28b). There are numerous ways to take that. It could merely mean that man was in charge of *controlling* the *growth* of the fish and the sea by fishing, and hunting. Yet, at this point, no animal had been slain because there had not yet been *sin*. Coupled with this is the fact that it appears that both Adam and Eve were *vegetarians* at this point. They did *not* eat meat. Because of these things, it is doubtful that they were supposed to control the growth of fish and animals through *killing*.

Could it have been possible that Adam and Eve had the ability to walk on water or even float or glide into the air? Again, it may sound preposterous to us because we can do neither of these things. Yet, if man was originally given the charge to have dominion over the *fish* and the *birds*, how was that worked out?

Was Adam able to communicate with the animal world so that they understood him? Did he possess the ability to walk out onto the water so that he was in a better vantage point to do so, getting closer to fish?

Again, these are guesses, so please do not make the mistake of thinking that this is to be accepted as *dogma*. It is not. However, like everything else in this book, we are merely looking at *possibilities* and those possibilities may give us greater insight into how things work in the spiritual realm.

If any of this was true for Adam, this would make his fall from grace that much more painful. Imagine having the ability to walk on water, or float into the air as a natural part of your existence, then after the fall, it is *gone*. Missler indicates that right after the fall God may have changed atmospheric conditions and introduced entropy as well.

Nonetheless, the animals that once trusted you and obeyed your voice are now *afraid* of you. The ground so easily tilled before there was sin, now caused tiredness and fatigue, along with sweat and pain.

Jesus' ability to do what to us seems *supernatural*, or *paranormal*, may in essence be because His body was a *resurrected* body perfectly fitted for the spiritual realm *after* we die. It is obvious from Paul that the spiritual realm is filled with entities (powers, dominions and powers), that have the ability to fight with other entities (cf. Ephesians 6:12; Daniel 10), and even hold them at bay.

We see this in the case of Daniel 10 when it took Gabriel three weeks or 21 days to arrive to him. This is in spite of the fact that Gabriel headed to Daniel as soon as Daniel began praying.

Gabriel shared with Daniel that the Prince of Persia kept him from arriving quickly. It was only when Michael the Archangel came to Gabriel's aid that the Prince of Persia was overcome by the additional power of Michael, which allowed Gabriel to go on his way.

It is also interesting to note that Gabriel indicated that he knew that he would *again* come up against this Prince of Persia as he traveled *back* to God's throne. Why Gabriel could not take another way is not explained, but from the text, it appears that there was only *one* way Gabriel *could* take to get back to God's throne.

By the way, it becomes clear from Revelation that angels vary in size and ability. In Revelation 5:2, John states, "*And I saw a **strong** angel proclaiming with a loud voice, Who is worthy to open the book, and to loose the seals thereof?* (emphasis added) In another instance, John says, "*And I saw another **mighty** angel come down from heaven, clothed with a cloud: and a rainbow was upon his head, and his face was as it were the sun, and his feet as pillars of fire,*" (Revelation 10:1, emphasis added).

GOD'S PROTECTIVE HEDGE

"The angel of the LORD encampeth round about them that fear him, and delivereth them,"
- Psalm 34:7

God's protective hedge keeps out what He does not allow in!

Many times in the book of Revelation, angels are simply referenced as angels. Every so often, John refers in specific terms to one angel or another as standing out from the multitude. This particular angel just referenced in Revelation 10:1 seems to be a very large angel because of his ability to put one foot on the earth and one on the sea.

Elisha provides other examples. At one point, he prayed that God would open the eyes of a young man to the spiritual realm because the young man was very fearful. The Lord answered, opening the young man's eyes and he saw multitudes of angelic forces seemingly prepared for battle (cf. 2 Kings 6).

These situations provide us with a look *behind* the curtain. Granted, for the most part, they are merely glances, or quick looks, but nonetheless, they offer *information* and *insight*.

Of course, we are also familiar with the man Job and the situation that occurred in the heavenly realm when Satan came before God's throne. It may be that this particular situation offers us the greatest look at not only what happens behind the veil, but Satan's ability to create, or at least make things happen. It was there as Satan stood before God's throne that God Himself brought up the subject of Job to

Satan. Satan wasted no time in claiming that it was only due to the fact that God had built a hedge around Job that Job was as "perfect" as he was in life. Get rid of the hedge and watch Job fall!

Of course, what Satan is saying is that God protected Job *from harm,* by placing a wall of protection around him. From this accusation of the enemy of our souls, we can see that he had already likely *tried* to get at Job (or at least *wanted* to), but had been thwarted by the protection that God had placed around Job. God's elect angels *are* that protection.

Satan was now daring God to remove that protection and watch His servant Job fall. Apparently, what Satan did not realize at the time was that he (Satan) was actually being set up to see that God's man, Job was not about to fall and Satan would once again be defeated.

Do Not Touch Job

During the time that God allowed Satan to do whatever he wanted to do to Job's family, along with everything else that Job possessed, Satan was *not* allowed to *touch* Job at all. That was God's one rule for Satan, so Satan went off to create havoc. In no time, Satan had sent the Sabeans to attack and kill those in Job's household. Fire then fell from heaven, destroying Job's sheep and those who watched them. As if that was not enough, the Chaldeans came and further killed Job's servants and plundered his possessions. Finally, a tornado took the lives of his children. Then Satan merely stood back waiting for Job to curse God.

Upon hearing the news that all of this had occurred, not only did Job *not* curse God, but he immediately embraced these tragedies by stating that the Lord gives and the Lord takes away. Blessed be the name of the Lord (cf. 1:20-22). What a testimony! God blessed Job tremendously and he had been grateful for all of it. Now, much of this was gone from him, without warning, and he immediately began to praise the Lord (cf. 1 Thessalonians 5:18)!

Satan lost round one, but he was not ready to give up. He went back to the Lord and accused God of protecting Job's *body* and *mind*. If God removed *that* hedge, Job would surely fall. God grants Satan permission to do *to* Job what he will, *except* to take Job's life, which means Satan obviously has the ability to do so.

Do Not Kill Job

That was fine with Satan. He had plenty with which to work. The remainder of the book of Job reveals to us just how much Job suffered, and just what Satan was able to do to him. The following list is taken from the MacArthur Study Bible:

1. *Painful boils from head to toe (2:7, 13; 30:17)*
2. *Severe itching/irritation (2:7,8)*
3. *Great grief (2:13)*
4. *Lost appetite (3:24; 6:6,7)*
5. *Agonizing discomfort (3:24)*
6. *Insomnia (7:4)*
7. *Worm and dust infested flesh (7:5)*
8. *Continual oozing of boils (7:5)*
9. *Hallucinations (7:14)*
10. *Decaying skin (13:28)*
11. *Shriveled up (16:8; 17:7; 19:20)*
12. *Severe halitosis (19:17)*
13. *Teeth fell out (19:20)*
14. *Relentless pain (19:20)*
15. *Skin turned black (30:30)*
16. *Raging fever (30:30)*
17. *Dramatic weight loss (33:21)*[54]

One has to wonder, if Satan is capable of doing all of the things listed above, then he obviously is able to manipulate physical things in our

---

[54] MacArthur Study Bible, John MacArthur, Gen. Ed. (Thomas Nelson ©2006), 692

world, and manipulate *diseases* and other things *as they apply to human beings*.

Take some time to review the numbered list. Look up the verses associated with each malady. Consider what Satan is able to do to people, and *how* he is able to inflict *pain*. He obviously has the capacity to affect an individual *physically*, and mentally (as seen in his ability to create *hallucinations*).

What Satan is Able to Do
We know beyond doubt that Satan is capable of *affecting* and *infecting* human beings with all sorts of problems and maladies. In truth, this list may only scratch the surface of Satan's overall and total ability.

It is clear from Job, that Satan did not *possess* Job to accomplish these things either. He simply made them happen from *outside* of Job. How Satan achieved these things, we do not know. Did he create these problems with his thoughts, or with a word?

We also know that Satan is strictly under God's rule and can do nothing outside of God's divine and permissive will. While Satan *can* do all of these things, it is also unequivocally clear that Satan *has* the ability to take someone's life.

Does this power and ability come because of the fact that these beings are part of the spiritual realm, and as such, have power over our realm? It is possible. Even at that though, their power is completely under God's control.

In the book of Exodus, if we consider the plagues that God sent to Egypt, prior to the release of the children of Israel, we are again met with numerous events that are calculated to initially *suggest* that Satan is as strong as God. Of course, this is not the reality. In nearly every case, when Moses turned the Nile River to blood, the sorcerers in Pharaoh's court were able to do the same. In fact, they were able to match Moses point for point, with slight differences.

When Moses dropped his staff on the ground, it turned into a snake. The sorcerers were able to do the same thing, yet Moses' snake turned and *devoured* the other snakes.

The sorcerers were unable to duplicate a number of things and the Passover was one of them. This event was fully in God's hands. This is not to say that Satan cannot take life, because we know that he can. What this says though is that God specifically *allowed* Satan to use his power through Pharaoh's sorcerers to replicate the very things that God was doing. However, God always showed His *greater* strength with the Passover being the final act, of which Pharaoh could no longer say no to Moses and let the people leave.

Of course, we know that only a very short time later, Pharaoh mustered his troops and they all went after the Israelites (as God motivated them to do so). This brought the entire period of events to a complete climax, one in which Pharaoh and his armies were drowned in the Red Sea. As Paul states in Romans 9:17, "*For the scripture saith unto Pharaoh, Even for this same purpose have I raised thee up, that I might shew my power in thee, and that my name might be declared throughout all the earth.*"***

It is clear then, that what Satan does, he does because God *allows* him to do it. Though God has seemingly allowed Satan to retain all of his power and rank, Satan's activity is always limited by God's sovereign will.

If you are like me, it is no doubt difficult for to wrap your brain around this whole concept. How does a being who is *not* God, have these types of abilities in the spiritual realms, and how does that *look* or *work* itself out when he uses those powers? The spiritual realm surrounds us. The entities existing there remain separated from us by a thin *dimensional* wall.

The ability to penetrate that dimensional wall seemingly with ease, allowing them to create havoc, diseases, and other things as well, means that their ability to *manipulate* our physical world is not at all that difficult. If so, how difficult is it for them to *create* events that *seem* altogether *real* to us though may only be strong illusions?

The illustration on the next page helps us visualize the situation. We can see the bottom right hand corner shows a snippet of our planet. There are two men and running from what appears to be an approaching UFO, very large and looming. Above them is another type of UFO.

Could spirits within that realm create both, or at least the *illusion* of UFOs? Again, if they can manipulate physical things in our world, create diseases, famines, pestilences and other things, can it be difficult for them to create the *illusion* of a UFO flying at them? I don't think so, and I believe that this is *exactly* what they do.

This is not to say that everything people experience is an *illusion*. It *is* to say that *much* of it might very well be based on an incredibly *strong* illusion, an illusion so detailed, that it may *appear* to be real. Why would there be a need for demons or fallen angels to have to actual *create* something *physical* all the time? There would really be no need at all. If the event or scenario was created in such a way that it *felt* real, it *looked* real, and it *sounded* real, then to the brain it *is* real. Our brain reacts to stimulus virtually the same way, whether that stimulus comes from within the brain, or outside the brain.

Think about a situation that has occurred in your life in which someone did something that *incensed* you. You became very angry because of what they had done. As you continue to recall the situation, some of the same things you *felt* when it actually took place

BEINGS OF THE INTER-DIMENSIONAL KIND

©2010 F. DERUVO

(Spiritual Dimension)

(Our Earth Dimension)

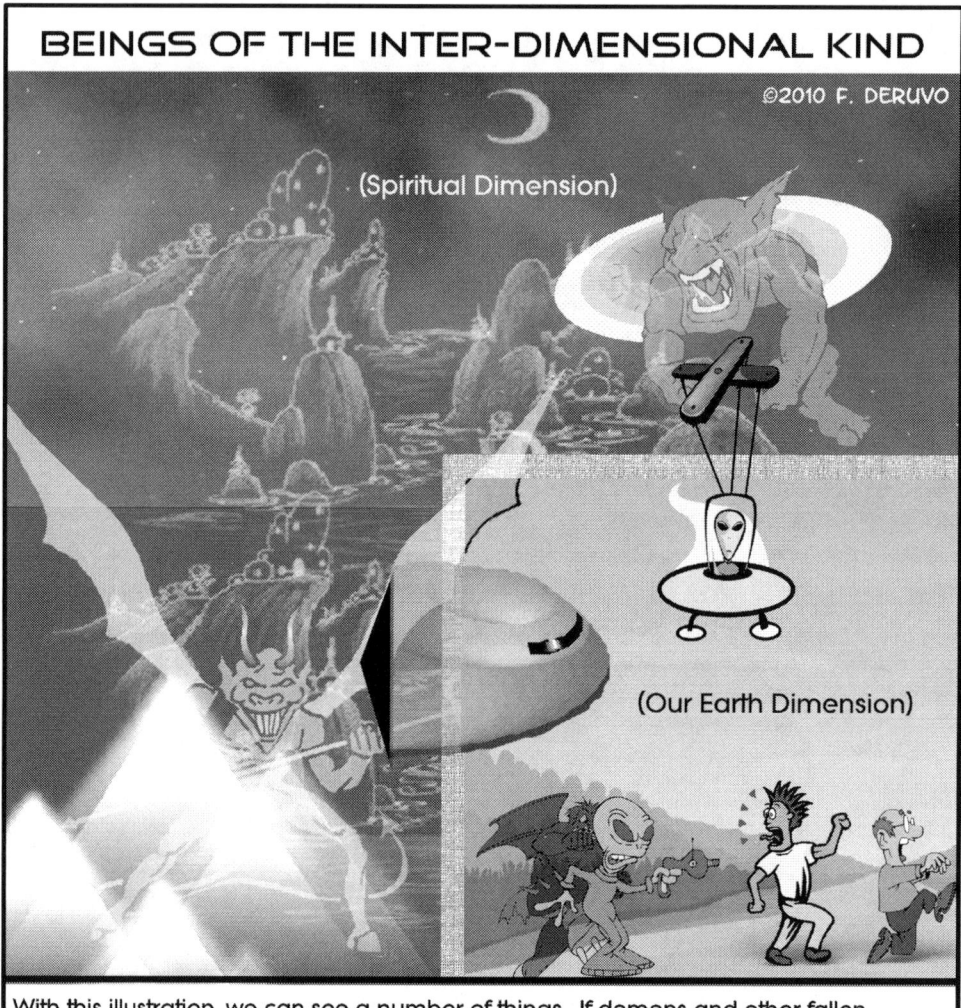

With this illustration, we can see a number of things. If demons and other fallen angels have tremendous power in their natural realm, what stops them from being able to manipulate the things in OUR realm, things that we cannot manipulate?

We see the one winged demon/fallen angel, pushing the front of a spaceship through the dimensional curtain. He also allows part of his wing to come through too. No one would know what that was, as it would simply look UFOish. Unable to see back through that curtain, we have no clue that it is part of his wing with the UFO merely a prop on a stick, so to speak. We also see a demon above the dimensional curtain, dangling a UFO down through the top of it.

In the final scenario, we see another winged demon on our side of the dimensional curtain masquerading as an alien who is pointing a space gun at two humans. Unable to see the demon behind the alien they are convinced that it is a real alien.

begin to come to the surface once again. If you dwell on it long enough, you will be re-enacting the situation in your brain, yet you *feel* as though you are actually *in* the situation as it happened, when it occurred the first time.

Conversely, consider an episode in your life that provided you a great deal of happiness. Do you feel yourself starting to react to it inside yourself as if it was happening now? That is because your brain *recreates* the memory as *reacts* to it as if it was real.

This is Your Brain

Your brain does not recognize the difference between something it experiences outside itself, or inside. People can react to things that are occurring in their brain, as if they were *physically* taking place. Our brain simply works this way.

This is actually what good actors do. They have learned over time to use their brain to help bring feelings to the surface. Feelings, which come to the surface, allow the actor to *be in the moment*. They are not *acting* at that point. They are *living* as if that moment was present for them because to their brain, it *is* happening at that moment. This is why some actors never look as if they are acting, while others always look as if they are acting. It is also, why some actors seem very weird or strange to us when not acting. Who are they today? Who are they now? Are they ever really just themselves? Do they even know who they are in actuality?

For those actors who mainly act in theater, there is a different style of acting. Normally, the gestures and expressions, as well as the volume of the voice are exaggerated in order that those seated in the back of the audience will be able to hear and see everything. This is done on purpose.

Take that same actor who is used to only acting in theater, and put them in front of a camera, and what you will see is someone who is *overacting.* They are used to acting in one venue, which does not translate to another automatically or with ease.

Quality movie and television actors must train themselves to *reduce* their expressions and gestures, the *closer* the camera gets. Even though they are still *in the moment*, they must adjust how much emotion they allow through their facial features, which the camera sees. The camera never lies. It sees when you are acting and when you are in the moment. As soon as the audience realizes it, they are also taken out of the moment, and they realized *"Oh, I'm in a theater, watching this!"* It may take a few moments to once again become absorbed in the movie or play, so that you forget that you are sitting in a theater seat, watching a movie or play unfold before you.

However, for any actor, the more real the emotion is for them *while* acting, the more they are simply living in that moment. In essence then, it *is* real, to both them and the audience.

The entities within the spirit world *know* how the human brain works and the complexity of our emotions stems from the brain's memory activity (from observation alone). Because of this, their ability to manipulate those things in our realm allows them to create *non-physical* realities that *appear* to us as actual because of how they are able to influence us through our brain waves and reactions.

It is not a great deal different from having a terrible nightmare, in which a person wakes up in a sweat, with their heart racing, and their pulse speeding along. The reaction that the body went through was due to the level of reality that the dream created.

If Satan is capable of creating hallucinations for Job, then it is obvious that he can do that to us. Job 7:14-15 states, *"Then thou scarest me with dreams, and terrifiest me through visions: So that my soul chooseth strangling, and death rather than my life."* Think about what Job is saying here. If his dreams and visions were so scary and terrifying to him that he wished for death, then is it possible that what Job saw might have been a peak into the spiritual realm? If not that, then he saw what Satan conjured up for him to see in any case. Those dreams and visions petrified poor Job!

At best, we can only guess about the specifics of the spiritual realm. The Bible gives us glimpses because we normally see through a dark veil. One day, the veil will lift and we will see and understand *all* of it.

***An excellent book providing tremendous archaeological evidence, insight, and research on the Israelite Exodus from Egypt is called *The Exodus Case*, by Lennart Moller.

Chapter 10

Here Is Where It Gets Weird

READY FOR OUR DATE?

E arlier in this book, Barbara Marciniak was quoted. Marciniak is author of *Bringers of the Dawn (Teachings from the Pleiadians).* Her book is an amazing revelation by spiritual entities from the other realm.

If one were to ask Marciniak who the entities are, she will tell you that they are highly advanced space aliens, who began as Pleiadians, but have grown to the point where they now refer to themselves as Pleiadians Plus. To quote Marciniak, *"The Pleiadians are a collective of extraterrestrials from the star system the Pleiades. They have been speaking through Barbara Marciniak since May 18, 1988; they say they were conceived on Harmonic Convergence and birthed in Athens, Greece, nine months later."*[55]

The entire book (allegedly) dictated to Marciniak who recorded and transcribed all of it, by the Pleiadians. I use the word allegedly, not because I do not believe it happened. I use it because I do not believe the entities that revealed these things to Marciniak are in fact, *Pleiadians* (or space aliens). I believe they are nothing more than fallen angels and Nephilim *demons*.

Ever since I began studying the Bible with respect to the End Times, or Last Days, I have always found it amazing that there are books *outside* of Christianity that the average Christian does not use in their study, which *can* offer insight. By this, I mean that, while we *know* beyond doubt that Satan lies, there is always truth mixed in with the error. What I have consistently found is that many of these books (such as *Bringers of the Dawn*), often refer to biblical events, but the events are turned upside down. Good is bad, black is white, yes is no and so on.

It should not have to be said that this kind of research opens one up to the anger and potential harassment of these entities. However, it should *also* be noted that they harass only as God *allows*. Being literally bathed with prayer and in constant communion with God is the only way to maintain that protection. If we become filled with a prideful or a know-it-all attitude, it only takes God to **allow** some type of harassment to occur before we realize that we have taken the wrong approach. Humbling approaching the throne of grace is needed.

I do not want to be accused of stating that anyone and everyone should enter this arena of research. I also do not want to be misunderstood to say that studying this area is no big deal. It *is* a big

---

[55] Barbara Marciniak, *Bringers of the Dawn* (Rochester: Bear & Co, 1992), 245

deal. What I *am* saying is that *if* the Lord leads, then never go there without the assurance of His protective presence. Go in His strength and in full trust of His faithfulness and promises. While the enemy of our souls can do us *no* harm unless God allows, we do *not* need to bring it on ourselves by taking God's protective hedge for granted.

It was in this mindset that I began reading through Marciniak's book and what I read was eye opening, to say the least. The entire point to *Brings of the Dawn* is to wake humanity up to the fact that the earth is heading toward a major *paradigm* shift. The reality that we experience *now* will be turned on its head as more and more people come to realize that, they are *gods*, and they have the ability to create their own realities.

You've heard it before? Of course, you have, but the essence of the book reveals the *steps* that these entities are revealing to humanity through people like Marciniak. Let me start at the beginning of her book and summarize it in chunks, quoting here and there when necessary.

Bringers of the Dawn: "Prime Creator"
In this first chapter called "Ambassadors Through Time," the Pleiadians introduce themselves to Barbara with the words, "*We are here. We are the Pleiadians, a collective of energy from Pleiades.*"[56] From this launching pad, these Pleiadians provide a detailed history of their species. They inform us how this planet came to be, and how *we* came to be on this planet.

Of course, it all began with the "Prime Creator." This Creator, while *not* one individual, contains a group of much higher energies, or entities, of which these Pleiadians would like to eventually merge with, at least for a time.

---

[56] Barbara Marciniak, *Bringers of the Dawn* (Rochester: Bear & Co, 1992), 3

They indicate that the *"veils around Earth were lifted at the time of the Harmonic Convergence,"*[57] which took place on August 16th to 17th 1987. Since these veils were, according to the Pleiadians, lifted out of the way, energy since then has been consistently going out to the outer areas of the cosmos. These beings *receive* that energy and then stepping it up so that it is increased. They increase it in order for humanity to more quickly progress to the next evolutionary plane in this planet's future history. Throughout the book, we are told repeatedly that a *"transition is about to occur, a dimensional shift that will lessen the density of the third dimension so that you will move in higher dimensions in which the body does not have such a solid state."*[58]

Sounds like they are describing when "he who restraineth" is taken out of the way. These Pleiadians insist that we *already* possess *all* the answers, deep within the recesses of our being. Isn't that nice? Unfortunately, we have been brainwashed into thinking that we need to look *outside* of ourselves. What is the one main lesson we are to learn? It is *"to realize your godhood."*[59]

Much of the remainder of this chapter centers on *why* we have been brainwashed and what needs to be done to free up our thinking. Even though we *think* we have free will, we do not, because we are constantly under the *control* of one group of entities or another, all of whom are vying to harness the energy that we *emit* from our bodies.

Of course, throughout this chapter (and the entire book itself), the Pleiadians emphasize that there are those on this planet who are *fear mongers*. These believe that the intrusion of space beings is reason to fear, yet the Pleiadians say that this is not true. Would they lie?

What is maintained throughout the book is that the Pleiadians are interested in *increasing* our understanding of reality. Apparently, we

---

[57] Barbara Marciniak, *Bringers of the Dawn* (Rochester: Bear & Co, 1992), 5
[58] Ibid, 5
[59] Ibid, 6

do not know what reality is in our world. They also indicate that *nothing* they tell us (through Marciniak) should ever be taken literally. Their words are designed to create images, which feed into the bigger picture.

The bigger picture is revealed as humans become more adept at avoiding the use of *logic*, replacing it with *feeling* and *intuition*. In fact, one of the dangers on this planet apparently has to do with the person *"who overdefines and tells you absolutes. It is important to hear many different opinions and many different stories. Listen to a person's story and see if **it feels right**."*[60] (emphasis added)

Probably the most startling revelation from the Pleiadians is the statement made regarding the consistency of their message. *"No matter what story we tell you today, we guarantee you that a year from now we will tell you a different story, because a year from now you will be able to comprehend things in a grander fashion. So the story will constantly evolve."*[61] That covers the bases for any error.

In chapter one alone, we have learned a number of very important things:

- *A major paradigm shift is going to occur*
- *Feelings and intuition are more valuable than logic*
- *Fearing the Pleiadians is not good because they want to help*
- *Their story will always be changing because truth is relative*

So much for absolutes! The Pleiadians have laid the groundwork for redefining what has always been accepted, at least in one form or another. By the way, it is not merely Marciniak who has published books like this either. Other individuals have also produced books said to be messages from aliens, and in large measure, the messages are very similar.

---

[60] Barbara Marciniak, *Bringers of the Dawn* (Rochester: Bear & Co, 1992), 10
[61] Ibid, 10

History Lessons Abound

Chapter 2 goes into much more depth regarding humanity's history and the Prime Creator's "journey." Anyone who is biblically literate will note the parallels between *Bringers of the Dawn* and the Bible. In fact, it almost becomes humorous the way the Pleiadians quote Scripture without *directly* quoting it verbatim, but usually by *implying* it in their verbiage to Marciniak, who may have no clue.

In this chapter, the connection lies in the fact that the Prime Creator allegedly created *creator gods*, who went out from the Prime Creator to experiment and experience the energy of Prime Creator. In other words, what were these creator gods able to accomplish with it? Prime Creator wanted to see what their results. Many hierarchies were created, which in turn became so complex that there were hierarchies within hierarchies.

Eventually, somewhere along the line, *the plan* was put together to create earth "*as an inter-galactic exchange center of information.*"[62] In effect then, Earth became a bit of a battleground between many forces – both dark and light – with one group gaining control for a time, and then that control changing hands to another group.

Following a group of skirmishes and battles, planet Earth fell into the hands of new owners and these new owners were apparently brilliant geneticists. They not only *created* life, but also apparently created humanity as quite a different creature from what we are today. "*The original human was a magnificent being whose twelve strands of DNA were contributed by a variety of sentient civilizations.*"[63] The new owners of earth changed humanity, making us far less than what we were originally created to be. Though our original DNA remained deep within our cells, it virtually lies dormant and unused. Could they be describing Adam and Eve?

---

[62] Barbara Marciniak, *Bringers of the Dawn* (Rochester: Bear & Co, 1992), 14
[63] Ibid, 16

The remainder of the chapter deals essentially with shamanism and chakras, mixed with scientific talk of helixes and other things related to DNA. This is the Pleiadians' attempt to explain how life *evolved* without saying that it evolved the way science has explained it to us.

There is No "One" God But Lots of Wormholes

Chapter 3 goes into great detail about gods – *what* they are and *who* they are, as far as we are concerned. Of course, humanity has it *wrong*. There is no *real* God at all. We have made the mistake of calling super-advanced entities "God" because of what they can do, compared to what we cannot. The Pleiadians state, "*Your history has been influenced by a number of light beings whom you have termed God. In the Bible, many of these beings have been combined to represent one being, when they were not one being at all, but a combination of very powerful extraterrestrial light-being energies.*"[64]

The Pleiadians assure us through Marciniak, that there is no form of literature available to us that adequately explain the nature of these beings. Right off the bat, we know that they are saying the Bible is not an authoritative source.

The Pleiadians tell us is that the most important *vibration* is one of *love*. They refer to it as the "food of love" and the necessity of getting back to it. If the entire universe speaks the *love frequency*, then we will go from our earth, to *seed* (start) life on other planets. Why does this remind me of the *1970s*, or *Mormonism*?

It is also interesting to note that the Pleiadians point out that human beings were originally *multi-dimensional*, having the ability to travel from one dimension to another at will. They want us to get back to that point. Apparently, though, some of the creator gods took this reality from us. We have inadvertently referred to some of these creator gods as *the* God, yet the Pleiadians are careful to point out

---

[64] Barbara Marciniak, *Bringers of the Dawn* (Rochester: Bear & Co, 1992), 24

*"God with a big G has never visited this planet as an entity. God with a big G is **in all things**."*[65] (emphasis added)

What must *not* be missed is that individuals like Barbara Marciniak accept whatever these Pleiadians state as the *gospel*. It is the truth, and nothing that does *not* feel right *can* be the truth.

Repeatedly, the Pleiadians implore humanity to learn to go only by *emotion*, *feeling*, and *intuition*. Toss logic out as unreliable.

In fact, the Pleiadians find ways to turn everything around, even pointing out that the entities we often refer to as the *powers of darkness*, are not factually bad at all. *"Be kind when you speak of the forces of darkness. **Do not speak as if they are bad**. Simply understand that they are uninformed..."*[66] (emphasis added)

Chapter 3 also teaches us about the subject of *portals* or *wormholes*. We have all heard of these, because they tend to be a staple in many Sci-Fi shows and movies. We are told that these portals are used to move from one dimension to another. This ties in with what we learned from Lynne Dickie's interview with L. A. Marzulli. She also spoke of wormholes in the sky that made her think of an ant farm.

Would you like to know where the biggest portal is now on the earth? It is over the Middle East. Why? Simply due to the fact, that so many wars have taken place there by entities from numerous dimensions. The portal itself is roughly 1,000 miles across and there is constant activity occurring.

If all this talk of wormholes and portals to other worlds are true, then it would certainly make sense why Gabriel told Daniel that he knew that when he returned to God's throne, he would have to fight the Prince of Persia again. Since the question was posed earlier in the

---

[65] Barbara Marciniak, *Bringers of the Dawn* (Rochester: Bear & Co, 1992), 27
[66] Ibid, 31

book about why Gabriel had to go back to God's throne the same way, the existence of wormholes, portals or some type of doorway connecting our realm with the heavenly realm makes a good deal of sense. Can I be dogmatic about it? No, and I do not *intend* to be. It is an interesting concept, and that is all.

As the book progresses, it gets more interesting because of the spin that the Pleiadians put on what we understand in biblical terms.

Light and Dark Forces: Two Sides of the Same Coin
In this chapter, the Prime Creator is credited with directly creating both the dark *and* the light forces. The dark forces did not come to exist as dark forces by *falling* from grace. They were created that way, according to the Pleiadians.

This chapter also introduces the concept of *worship*, as humanity looks toward something or someone *new* to worship. The Pleiadians point to a *coming* event or *person* that will be shown to the world *holographically*, as an *insert*, which will be understood as a *"new god to worship."*[67] The chapter ends with the warning about endeavoring to *feel*, instead of think. Emotions are *superior* to logic and thought.

What I gather from this book is that these fallen angels and Nephilim demons have a difficult time *feeling*, if there is any truth that can be gleaned from these thoughts. In fact, the Pleiadians tell us that the *more* we use our feelings, the *greater* the energy *output*. The greater the energy output, the more energy is available for the Pleiadians to consume. Again, if any of this is true, then it makes the concept of *demonic possession* that much more clear. Other authors have also noted this that demons seem to thrive on doing things while inside a person that causes the individual *harm*. To the demon though, it does not matter if the feeling created is *good* or *bad*. What matters is that they *feel*. The stronger the emotion, the more the demons gain

---

[67] Barbara Marciniak, *Bringers of the Dawn* (Rochester: Bear & Co, 1992), 44

from it. If they at one point actually had bodies of flesh, prior to the Flood, but have since been roaming the atmospheric heavens without a body, the desire to be in some type of body must cause them to react as a drug addict yearning for the next fix. It must be overwhelming at times, so great is their desire to feel and emote *physically*.

DNA Lessons

DNA discussion and teaching, and confirmation (or is it repetition) that we were once multi-dimensional beings is again brought up in this chapter. This chapter also begins the discourse on *sexuality* and the Pleiadians begin to turn things upside down in that area as well. They question *who* made the rules about sexuality. They explain *why* people currently believe they need to be married in order to experience marital intercourse, and why there is the continuing belief that homosexuality is wrong. In point of fact, it all boils down to *love*, and it does not matter if two human beings are married or if they are in a same-sex relationship. If *love* is there, that is the *highest* frequency, which accelerates the evolution of this planet. This planet needs to become one huge love fest in order to evolve. Funny how history shows that falling to this level (or lack) of morality has *destroyed* every previous once great civilization!

Sexuality Again

This one deals with more history and the fact that skeletal forms will be uncovered, of creatures that are far different from what we have grown to expect in the fossil record. The subject of sexuality is also brought up again in this chapter. The emphasis again is on loving the individual you are *with*, not worrying about the old accepted standards that have been pumped into our subconscious.

Mutli-dimensional

This chapter goes into more detail about our original bodies, which were multidimensional. The Pleiadians emphasize that we need to toss logic, and replace it with feeling and emotion in order to get back to that point. So, all you people who use and enjoy the facet of logic, fuggedaboutit! Talk about repeating yourself...

Martial Law is Not as Bad As Controlling the Consciousness

This chapter opens with this grand statement. *"The ultimate tyranny in a society is not control by martial law. It is control by the psychological manipulation of consciousness, through which reality is defined so that those who exist within it do not even realize that they are in prison. They do not even realize that there is something outside of where they exist. We represent what is outside of what you have been taught exists."*[68]

That is an interesting statement because these entities are the ones who want to *enslave* and *control* all of humankind by having us do things *their* way. Due to the lies of these entities however, many will embrace the error and believe the lie.

This chapter also deals with the issue of abortion and the Pleiadians assure humanity that *"Those who find their lives taken by accident or violence select it."*[69] To believe and accept that as truth means a total disregard for human life, which is where our society has been heading for some time. That is the way of reincarnation though.

Holographic Images from the Sky and the Art of Control

This chapter segues into one of the major lifestyle changes that took place in our century, and that was the invention of the *moving picture*. Movies *can* present a picture of life that way it *should* be, or the way people *want* it to be, or the way it *actually* exists. The Pleiadians liken movies on earth to the technology that aliens have in space, which is the *holographic image*. Of this, our Pleiadian friends tell us that because these space aliens are so far ahead of earthlings in technology, *"it is quite easy to hoodwink human beings."*[70] Of

---

[68] Barbara Marciniak, *Bringers of the Dawn* (Rochester: Bear & Co, 1992), 87
[69] Ibid, 93
[70] Ibid, 97

course, the Pleiadians would *never* do that, my goodness. Perish the thought. No, they refer to mischievous creator gods who for one reason or another, feel the need to play games with us, or keep us controlled by their programs and for their purposes.

The Pleiadians explain further that the holograms, or "holographic inserts," as they call them have been used a number of times throughout human history. This has been for the purpose of guiding or directing history in another direction from where it seemed to be moving. The issue of *control* again comes to the fore.

What is fascinating is that while the Pleiadians speak of wanting humans to be *free* of all control, they share with us many ways in which we *have* been apparently controlled, and are *still* controlled. In fact, the very book itself is a means of controlling us by making humanity believe that the Pleiadians' ways are the best and we should aspire *to* them, and only them. The trouble is that no one I know of in the New Age has ever taken the time to question this truth. They simply accept it, like lambs to the slaughter.

Interestingly enough, many of the holographic inserts have been used during *UFO* events, of all things. Would you believe it? Who would have ever thought? Tsk, tsk, tsk.

"Holographic experiences, especially viewing in the sky are set up to **influence a large group of people at once***. Many though not all, UFO sightings have been holographic inserts. There have been holographic inserts of one individual, designed in many fashions, projected simultaneously in many different cultures. That is why some of Earth's religious stories are parallel from one corner of the world to another when there was no physical contact."*[71] (emphasis added)

If there is *any* truth here, then this also answers Jacques Vallee and others about the reality of these UFO sightings. It also provides a

---

[71] Barbara Marciniak, *Bringers of the Dawn* (Rochester: Bear & Co, 1992), 98

reason *why* a ton of people can be looking in the same sky at the same time, with only *some* of the people present seeing a UFO, or whatever is there.

Inserts and Reality

Regarding these holographic inserts, the Pleiadians assure us that they look just like 3-D reality. These 3-D holographic movies are literally inserted into our history and of course, appear to be part of the historical action that has taken place. They are so real that they are extremely difficult to recognize as artificial. Of course, you would probably never guess that many of these holographic inserts are focused on the Middle East, would you? The Pleiadians indicate that as time progresses, "*Some of the grand events will be very legitimate, and some of them will be inserts designed to move the consciousness of humanity toward the **one world order** to be controlled.*"[72] (emphasis added) Sounds like *control* to me.

So how best to discern these holographic inserts? Is there any sure way to know which events are *authentic*, and which are *inserts*? Absolutely, and it is by using our *feeling* or *intuition*! Would you like to learn of at least one major holographic insert used to hoodwink humanity? The Pleiadians explain. "*An example of a holographic insert that was put on the planet in the past to change the course of history is **the crucifixion of Christ**. The drama that was played out and passed on historically to you is **not** the reality that the Christed One came in to play. A version of this entity's life was molded and designed in a holographic entertainment movie, which was then inserted and played out as if it were real.*"[73] (emphasis added)

You know, ever since Satan prompted the crowds to scream for Christ's blood, I'm certain he regrets doing so. Imagine if Christ had not died by the cross. We would have no salvation. Satan tried to kill

---

[72] Barbara Marciniak, *Bringers of the Dawn* (Rochester: Bear & Co, 1992), 98
[73] Ibid, 101

Christ ahead of time bypassing the cross, but failed. I'm not sure he really understood the full portent of Christ's death on the cross.

The Pleiadians assure us that there may be *other* holographic inserts, such the Second Coming of Christ, possibly. Interesting choice. Of these holographic inserts, we should be *extremely* careful *not* to believe that they are real. Wow, what a set up.

Look, Up in the Sky, It's *SUPER*-CONSCIOUSNESS!
In this chapter, we learn that the *Bringers of the Dawn* literally carry the sun's rays, along with light and knowledge to this planet. Of course, *human beings* are the Bringers of the Dawn. Who would have guessed? Are you thinking of a song made famous by the 5th Dimension years ago?

The remainder of the book goes back and forth between assuring us that things will get *wild*, to warning us that it is *imperative* that we connect with our super-consciousness in order to stave off the effects of the malcontents (*read: Christians – ed.*) on this planet. By doing this, we will be able to *create* our own reality a la the Matrix.

After reading books like this, is it any wonder that movies like the Matrix Trilogy were made and received as well as they were? We *must* spend time validating ourselves, telling ourselves how much we *love* ourselves. We are *good*, we are *fine*, we are *god*, and we are *free*. Once we become intuitively familiar with this, we will become closer to the *exalted self* that the Pleiadians are apparently looking to occur within us, because this world needs many exalted selves (or is that *exalted slave?*). An *unexalted* self simply will not do.

Throughout the book, biblical terms and phrases flow, like "pillar of light," which of course has nothing to do with *the* Pillar of Light that was God, used to guide and protect the Israelites as they moved through the wilderness. The pillar of light spoken of by the

Pleiadians is for *our* use, *our* benefit, and to *free* us from the control we currently live under, so that we come under their control.

Repeatedly, we read that we need to get rid of *logic*, and go with *feelings*, *emotions*, and *intuition*. Logic confuses. Emotions and intuition free us.

As an aside here, it makes much more sense now when I consider some of the movements that have taken the visible Church by storm. The Charismatic movement, Latter Rain, the Laughing Revival, and many other events as well, all of them have emphasized *feelings* and *emotion*. Adherents are told not to question it, just go with it.

There is *nothing* wrong with emotions, as long as they do not *guide* us. This was the problem with Eve apparently (from the Pleiadians' perspective). According to them, women were created to rely on their emotions and intuition. Men were created to be more logical. This says *nothing* about intelligence, by the way. It simply points out differences between genders on an emotional level. If this is true, then it certainly makes sense why Satan went to *Eve* and not to *Adam*. Eve fell because she relied on feelings and intuition.

The Rapture?!
Several times in *Bringers of the Dawn*, the Pleiadians speak of an upcoming event that is strikingly similar to the Rapture. Those who are unable to change will be removed from the earth. This may serve to wake the remaining people of this planet up, so that they will realize the importance of *merging* with the Earth's frequency. It is only as more and more people learn to create their own reality that the planet itself will change.

At one point, the Pleiadians describe nearly *verbatim* what Christ described in the Olivet Discourse regarding the coming *birth pangs*. "*It will seem that a great chaos and turmoil are forming, that nations are rising against each other in war, and that earthquakes are happening more frequently. It will seem as if everything is falling apart and cannot be put back together. Just as you sometimes have rumblings and quaking in your lives as you change your old patterns and move into new energies, Earth is shaking itself free, and a certain realignment or adjustment period is to be expected."*[74]

Watchers in the Sky

The Pleiadians then attempt to explain something that they *admit* is difficult to explain. Of course, the reason it is difficult is that it is apparently *beyond* our actual ability to grasp since we exist in this dimension. They speak of a major change coming over the earth, with many *observers in the sky*, taking note.

Apparently, though, not all human beings will be able to change *with* the Earth, and they will actually be leaving the planet. Of these, the Pleiadians indicate, *"The people who leave the planet during the time of Earth changes do not fit here any longer, and they are stopping the harmony of Earth. When the time comes that perhaps twenty million people leave the planet at one time, there will be a tremendous shift in consciousness for those who are remaining. When a large group passes over together, they create an impact upon the consciousness of those who remain."*[75]

Another reference to a Rapture is indicated by the Pleiadians in chapter sixteen. What is interesting though, in their version this time, it is for those who *have* been able to make the change. It is interesting how Satan attempts to cover his bases. The first "rapture" means that those who cannot change will be taken. The next "rapture" (which will never happen, but keeps people coddled), is for those who *have* been able to make the change. This gives them something for which to look forward.

---

[74] Barbara Marciniak, *Bringers of the Dawn* (Rochester: Bear & Co, 1992), 166
[75] Ibid, 167

The 144,000

Chapter 17 speaks of *"144,000 members of the spiritual hierarchy who are infused in the gridwork of the planet at this time. Each master has its own seal that represents one portion of the Language of Light, and you have 144,000 seals of energy that will eventually be infused within your being."*[76]

That is fascinating. Who hasn't heard of the 144,000? Well here is the "real" take on it. Forget what the Bible says because this number really has nothing to do with Jewish individuals at all. It has to do with *energy* that will be infused within. I'm in awe. Are you in awe? I'm in awe. Energy. Neato. Who does not need more energy?

The Coming Implants

We also learn of geometric *implants* that will be planted *within* people. This *"implant comes when you truly commit yourself to what was formerly not possible."*[77] Could this be referring to the mark of the beast here? Hmmm, let me think. Apparently, these geometric implants come in a number of different shapes. One of the forms is a pyramid structure. Since the pyramid represents a *"great unity of consciousness."*[78]

To the Pleiadians, the pyramid is a perfect structure. Moreover, the sphere and spiral will also be implant forms, as well as parallel lines and the cube. Last, but not least, is the five-sided Merkabah. This is said to represent the *"figure of the human being in its most unlimited state – the totally free human...it is the human design without any limitations."*[79] That is just *swell*, isn't it? Why, it is downright crackerjack! Of course, we know the Merkabah, as God's chariot in Ezekiel 1:4-26.

---

[76] Barbara Marciniak, *Bringers of the Dawn* (Rochester: Bear & Co, 1992), 182
[77] Ibid, 183
[78] Ibid, 182
[79] Ibid, 182

Reading this book is truly a detailed instruction manual for the New Age. The fact that these entities *imply* events that the Bible says will occur (or have occurred on earth), says a good deal.

Obviously, we cannot take what they say as *truth*. Taken overall though, it becomes clear that these entities are not only *familiar* with the Bible, but likely know it better than we do! They use this knowledge to twist the truth into their lie in order to deceive millions upon millions of people on this planet.

It's a Wormhole, Chester

Whether wormholes or portals exist or not is beside the point. These entities are explaining things in terms that we understand, how they are able to travel to and from the earth at such great speeds, for instance.

They have taken events of the Bible, and twisted them so that *their* explanation of those events seems *plausible*. They *know* that this world is moving to a *one-world order*, because this is what they tell people like Barbara Marciniak and others. That part is obviously true. They know that a *one-world leader* is coming up through the ranks, and is probably here now even as I write this, yet they turn it around to mean that this individual is *favorable*, one in which the world awaits. That part is also true (about the one-world ruler). The fact that he will be benevolent and good is *hogwash*. The event itself is going to occur, and that individual will walk onto the world's stage, to captivate the masses, which he will eventually subjugate and *control* (there's that word again).

In our next and final chapter, we will do our best to wrap all of this up, taking into consideration the views of Vallee, Marzulli, Marciniak, and others. Where is this all leading? Interestingly enough, whether we get our information from the Bible (the obviously preferred place), or from Vallee or Marciniak, the truth is that it all appears to be two sides of the *same coin*.

It is like reading the story of Little Red Riding Hood, from the *wolf's* perspective. It is the same story, but with a *twist*. It would appear that this is exactly what Satan has been busy doing over the centuries; creating *alternate* meanings for God's plan and purposes. What else does he have, since we know that God's will and purposes *will* come to completion?

The Real Reason the Wolf Chased Red (according to the wolf)!

I WISH THAT GIRL WOULD STOP WALKING THROUGH MY GARDEN EVERY TIME SHE GOES TO HER GRANDMOTHER'S HOUSE! SHE IS RUINING MY VEGETABLES!!

OH NO, THE WOLF AGAIN! WHY DOES HE KEEP FOLLOWING ME?

©2010 F. DERUVO

Chapter 11

Where Is It Headed?

Both Jacques Vallee and L. A. Marzulli (as well as many others), offer tremendous insight into the UFO phenomenon; the former from a skeptical or humanistic perspective and the latter from a Christian perspective. In that sense, both views are worthwhile and beneficial because of the *comparisons* alone.

For Vallee, who clearly does *not* believe that these beings are demonic, or spiritual entities, but physical beings who are able to travel *between* dimensions, his conclusions lead him to believe that these beings are *toying* with us, that they are not here for any good purpose. From his research, he has concluded that they obviously have the ability to *maim* or *kill*, having allegedly done so at various times. These beings can be here one moment, then *gone* the next leaving no sign of their presence, though sometimes they *do* leave a physical sign.

People seeing the same UFO event might not see the same thing. These beings have also *controlled* various aspects of people's lives, often to *no* beneficial purpose. For Vallee then, the results are clear. These beings have the power and ability to destroy earth and us, so *why don't they do that*? Why don't they just fly in or land and take us over? Why do they allegedly need to *infiltrate* society by creating carefully engineered human (hybrid) replicas *first*?

Vallee's conclusions are (emphasis added):

1. *"The total number of close encounters far **exceeds** the requirements for a sophisticated survey of our planet.*
2. *The appearance of the UFO operators is overwhelmingly **humanoid**; they **breathe** our air and display recognizable **emotions**. Not only does this make an extraterrestrial origin very dubious, but it implies that the operators are **not making use of genetic engineering** to optimize a space mission, as interstellar travelers presumably would under the extraterrestrial hypothesis model.*
3. *The reports regarding abductions display behavioral patterns on the part of the operators that contradict the idea of scientific, medical, or genetic experiments. Simpler, more effective methods are already available in earth-based science to accomplish all the alleged objectives of these aliens.*
4. *The patterns of close encounters, contacts, and abductions are **not specific to our century**, contrary to what most American ufologists have assumed. In fact, it is difficult to find a culture that does* not *have a tradition of little people that fly through the sky and abduct humans. Often they take their victims into spherical settings that are evenly illuminated, and they subject*

them to various ordeals that include operations on internal organs and astral trips to unknown landscapes. Sexual or genetic interaction is a common theme in this body of folklore.

5. *Both the UFOs and their operators are able to **materialize** and **dematerialize** on the spot and to **penetrate physical obstacles**. The objects are able to **merge together** and to **change shape** dynamically."[80]*

Summing Valle Up

All of the above is extremely fascinating to say the least and I would agree with him on nearly all points. Concisely, Vallee has concluded that there have been excessively many encounters necessary if the aliens were simply conducting *surveys*. He further finds that the large majority of aliens already *resemble* human beings. That and their ability to breathe our air and show recognizable emotions place a huge question mark over the whole drama. Why do these aliens appear so much like humans? Vallee also seems to believe there is something going on but the *scientific*, *medical*, and *genetic* experimentation by these beings *masks* their true motivation.

Throughout human history, there appears to be a *through* line of alien encounters and abductions, not merely those connected with our current century. Finally, the ability of these beings to materialize and dematerialize at will and pass through physical objects suggests that these particular beings have control *over*, or the ability to *disregard* the scientific laws of our realms. If that is true, that alone directly contradicts their alleged need to wait, or to infiltrate society with human replicas slowly over time before they can obtain full control of this planet.

Regarding his own findings, he states, *"As an alternative to the extraterrestrial hypothesis, I propose to regard the UFO phenomenon as a physical manifestation of a form of consciousness that is alien to*

---

[80] Jacques Vallee, *Confrontations* (Ballantine Books: New York 1990), 131

humans but is able to coexist with us on the earth."[81] Though Vallee himself does not arrive at the same conclusion I do, what he surmises seems to point to beings of a quasi-*physical* nature, related to a consciousness that is best suited to *their* natural environment, which we would call the *spiritual realm*. Their quasi-*physical* nature allows them to travel inter-*dimensionally*.

Jesus Travels Inter-Dimensionally

We have discussed aspects of Jesus' life, and particularly His post-resurrection appearances in which there was virtually no difficulty for Him to pass through solid objects, or to disappear from among men instantly. Unless these attributes are reflective of deity *only*, it would appear that a body that is *post-death* or *post-resurrection* is one *unaffected* by the physical and scientific laws of *this* realm.

If these alleged space aliens can *also* appear and disappear, as well as travel *through* objects, then it would show that this ability is *not* relegated to God only, therefore it is *not* solely a characteristic of deity. Of course, these beings could be creating the *illusion* that they are doing this without actually doing it. That is always possible.

For Marzulli, the results of his research have led him to a completely different conclusion from Vallee as well, summed up best in his interview with Joe Jordan. Jordan is a Christian, and came to his own conclusions regarding the entire alien phenomenon after years of careful researched. According to Marzulli, Joe began researching in 1995, specifically in the area of abduction occurrences.

After spending hours and hours reading interviews and transcripts, as well as viewing videos with fellow researchers, Jordan concluded that the individuals who had allegedly been abducted all shared symptoms of having gone through something *terrible*. For them, it had been very real. The results of these experiences left the people

---

[81] Jacques Vallee, *Confrontations* (Ballantine Books: New York 1990), 131

changed and not necessarily for the better. He defers to Vallee here in referring to the results of these experiences as creating *reality transformations*.

Lives changed for many of the people who had experienced abductions or contact with aliens. They were not good things, though in many cases, it was difficult for them to *discern* at the time of the experience.

Probably one of the most important things Jordan noticed regarding these people was that *"their worldviews as they had been raised were changing. Many were becoming involved with metaphysical or New Age practices as a source of answers for their experience. This was a new area for us, as we were looking at this from an objective investigative point of view as MUFON (Mutual UFO Network – editor) had trained us. There seemed to be a conditioning process going on with the experiencers. Many of the signs were pointing to brainwashing techniques to accomplish this. Another thing to look at is the alleged communication from the entities. The message is usually* **an anti-Judeo-Christian message: Jesus is not who we think he is,** *they are our creators; the Bible is not the inerrant word of God. Why would these entities go through the effort to convince us of this when all the other religions of the world don't even agree with each other? What is so important about the Judeo-Christian message that they want to make us believe it's not true?"*[82] (emphasis added)

That is an excellent question, one deserving an answer. We must consider the fact that the messages these aliens bring to us are:

- *Overwhelmingly New Age*
- *Anti-Christian*
- *Anti-Jesus-as-God*
- *Designed to cause people to look within for their answers*

---

[82] L. A. Marzulli, *The Alien Interviews* (Spiral of Life, 2009)

- *Designed to ultimately teach that each person is god*

Warning! Warning, Danger Will Robinson!

All of this says something, which should literally *shout* a warning to the Christian, a warning that can*not* be ignored. Something is happening that *looks* as if it has been in the works for centuries. Things behind the dimensional curtain have been and are moving to a unified conclusion *on this planet.*

With all of the recorded interviews, the photographic and video evidence and the messages allegedly channeled by these beings through human hosts, it becomes clear that it is all moving to the same point. That point will bring about the Antichrist, and his one-world rule, over which he will exercise absolute imperialism, as Arnold Fruchtenbaum states in his book, *Footsteps of the Messiah.*

It does not matter if we are talking about the New Age itself, the New Age *within* the visible Church (Emergent Church), Tarot Cards, Meditation, Pyramid Power, Rock Music, Self-Help Books and Conferences, Crystal Balls and Fortune Tellers, Tai Chi, Reiki, religions like Hare Krishna, Buddhism, Islam, Aliens, or anything else that falls under the *paranormal* or *New Age.*

All of these things *originate* with Satan. All of it leads to the same climax, with a *one-world government* and a *one-world leader*, who will be *Satan's* man for that time, as Satan prepares to fight against the God of the Bible. Satan *seems* to have left no stone unturned in his efforts to *dominate* the very Creation that God made and that Satan is actually part of. Satan acts as if he always existed, yet he was in fact, created, and his puny attempts to remove God from His throne make Satan a usurper! In spite of what he believes to be true, Satan is *not* self-made. He *is* self-destroyed because of his own actions and choices!

All From <u>One Source</u> to Fulfill <u>One Purpose</u>

Antichrist   Israel

Satan

Many Paths – All But One Lead to Destruction

Satan has provided something for everyone. Even atheists and certainly agnostics are finding a way to be involved in the New Age movement *without* having to believe in any god at all. They have no clue that they are in fact, worshiping Satan! In fact, not one individual involved in any of the activities or movements noted on the chart shown on the previous page has a clue as to who is actually behind *whatever* it is they think they believe in. They have come to believe **the lie** that they are god! It is the **same** lie that Satan told Eve in the Garden of Eden, and people are **still** buying it!

When people toss logic to the wind, preferring to go by *feeling*, *emotion*, or *intuition*, this is the natural result. People who do this become very open and susceptible to any suggestions from the enemy. What else do they have to rely on for truth? Since they prefer their emotions to logic, it makes sense that they will succumb to lies from the enemy, who will also provide them with enough strong feelings, which they will judge are accurately assessing the situation *for* them.

In essence, we are speaking of a huge circle, with Satan as the instigator, and Satan as the line itself. It starts and stops with him, and the One who allows it so start, and carry forward is the same One *"whom the Lord shall consume with the spirit of his mouth, and shall destroy with the brightness of his coming,"* (2 Thessalonians 2:8b).

Everything about aliens smacks of Nephilim (demonic) and fallen angel activity. We have seen that the aliens are telling us that they have come to help us because they do not want to watch us destroy ourselves. We see their ships, we see the residue they leave behind when they land those ships, and we see the destruction they often leave in their wake (human lives, cattle mutilations, etc.).

Alien abductions seem to be increasing, or maybe people are more willing to discuss them, and if as Vallee states, they have visited our

192

Satan's Wheel of UN-Fortune

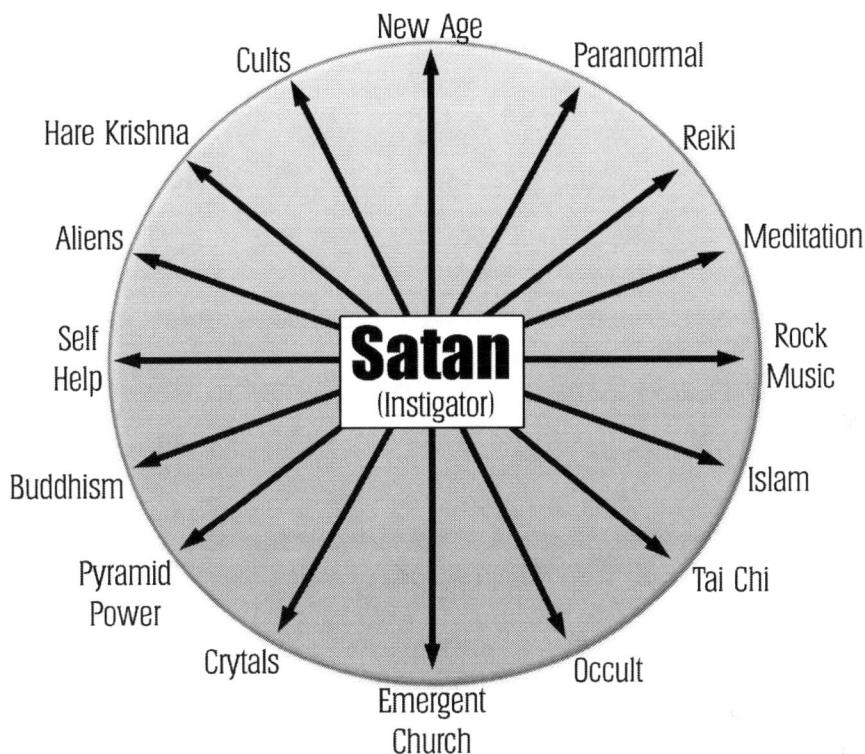

New Age
Cults
Paranormal
Hare Krishna
Reiki
Aliens
Meditation
Self Help

Satan
(Instigator)

Rock Music
Buddhism
Islam
Pyramid Power
Tai Chi
Crytals
Occult
Emergent Church

Satan has created something for everyone, in order to seduce and enslave. The above is only a sampling. What may not work for one, will work for another. All ways lead the world to the same ultimate climax, which is a one-world government, led by a one-world ruler. Satan will finally get his chance to rule over God's Creation, but not for long.

Welcome to *Your* Afterlife!

You're gonna HATE it here! Oh well...

(What, you were expecting aliens?)

COMPLAINT DEPT.

©2010 F. DERUVO

planet too much for it to simply be observation, then we must look for another answer.

If they are not here to destroy us outright or take over our planet, then all of this talk of interbreeding may be absolutely *nothing*. It may simply be part of their plan to *deflect* from the real purpose of their "visitations." Here are some things to consider:

Here to Help?

If they are in fact *aliens*, here to help us, then *why* have they not landed? Do they believe that we would attack them? They have no reason to fear because from what we know from Vallee's research, along with others like Marzulli, Cumby, Jacobs, and Missler, *nothing* we possess will cause them any concern. In fact, from the incidents investigated by Vallee, it would appear (if true) that a number of alien contacts with humans have resulted in instantaneous death and vaporization.

Why the Wait?

So if they are not waiting to reveal themselves because they may be afraid of *us* harming *them*, then what is the waiting all about? It *must* have to do with the fact of what Paul speaks of when he said that there is One who stands in the way. Until He stands to the side, allowing the coming wickedness to spread over the earth like a flood, these "aliens" will continue to provide excuse after excuse after excuse for why they are delayed in coming as our "savior."

It would be far easier to believe that these beings were actual space aliens, *if* they actually provided us with information that could aid our planet, like:

- *Cure for the common cold*
- *Cure for all cancers*
- *Cure for AIDS*
- *Helping us to eradicate hunger*

- *Improving our scientific endeavors for the good of humanity*
- *Eliminating the possibility of war anywhere on earth*

The above is just a small list. Certainly if these aliens *were* in fact higher, or more advanced beings, then providing the answers to the above listed problems should not be difficult at all. Yet, no such information is forthcoming regarding any of it.

All the information that the aliens have provided has to do with *a form of religion.* As has been stated, it is all *anti-Christian,* and *anti-Jesus.* According to Chuck Missler, some of these beings have stated that *they* are the ones who actually created us. We have it wrong. While the name of Elohim *is* correct, it represents *not* God, but a corporate group of *aliens* who came together to *seed* life on this planet. They are our creators, not the God of the Bible.

Wouldn't it be more *beneficial* to share some of their medical and scientific knowledge with us, before they decide to give us their own version of a Bible study lesson? Yet, they persist in providing the same *type* of religious instruction repeatedly. We are *all* gods and we just need to realize it. As soon as we *activate* our collective deity, this planet will move from this current evolutionary plane to the next, which supposedly is far better.

The reason we have not been able to move to that next level is due solely to:

- *A lack of understanding of our own inherent divinity*
- *Groups of "malcontents" or people with bad energy*

In the above two bullets, if the latter is dealt with, the former will automatically take care of itself. This is their thinking and their teaching to human beings who are willing to believe their lies. These human beings have either knowingly or unknowingly placed themselves in the line of fire by opening themselves up to demonic entities. These deceived human beings listen greedily at every word these beings speak. It does not matter how much New Age gobbledygook they spit out to humans everywhere. The very fact that these higher beings, or ascended masters are willing to condescend to us is reason enough to call them "master," as too many human beings are willing to do. This is tragic, not only because it gives Satan and his minions more room to work, having more numerous human channels to work through, but it also means the great possibility of another human soul delivered to hell upon their death.

Bait and Switch

"In retail sales, a bait and switch is a form of fraud in which the party putting forth the fraud lures in customers by advertising a product or service at an unprofitably low price, then reveals to potential customers that the advertised good is not available but that a substitute is. This use of this term has extended to similar situations outside of the marketing sense."[83]

The above definition of a bait and switch is as good as any. This type of sales method is probably most widely used in the sale of automobiles. A car dealer will put a car in an ad, in which they hope to bait the consumer into coming down to look at the car. Once there, the salesperson will direct them to a completely different car.

In effect, Satan has instructed those under his direct control within his kingdom to use *bait and switch* tactics on human beings. On one hand, whether it is *aliens*, or *ascended masters*, or *Maitreya*, a *dream* or *vision*, *Tai Chi, Reiki, Transcendental Meditation, Contemplative Prayer*, or anything else, *all* are designed to draw the "consumer" into Satan's web. They *think* that what they are going after is *legitimate* knowledge of the cosmos, and believe this knowledge will actually help them become an advanced individual, far superior to what they are now, moving toward *super-consciousness*. People may move

---

[83] http://en.wikipedia.org/wiki/Bait_and_switch

ahead with a bit of fear or trepidation, learning the "secrets" of the masters. Eventually, by following the prescriptive formulae of the New Age, they learn to harness the energy of their feelings, emotions, and intuition, while at the same time, ignoring the pull of logic.

After Satan and his cronies ensnare human beings this web of deceit, they begin reeling them in. The problem of course, is that *no human being* will ever understand that he or she just experienced the bait and switch, and will *not* understand it until it is too *late*. Unless God opens their eyes, the truth of their situation will not become apparent until *after* their *death*, which is too late.

There is nothing that has been revealed to human beings by these space entities that provides any reason to believe that they come in peace and that they want to help us *improve* our planet. What they want is to achieve Satan's goals, which include getting all humanity to believe *the lie* that we are individual gods. Once this occurs, it will be like taking candy from a baby for the Antichrist to achieve *his* goals. Antichrist will be welcome as the world's knight in shining armor, that most will not realize anything is wrong until it is far too late.

Workers of Deceit

We began this book with this Scripture reference, and I can think of no better way to end it.

"For such are false apostles, deceitful workers, transforming themselves into the apostles of Christ. And no marvel; for Satan himself is transformed into an angel of light. Therefore it is no great thing if his ministers also be transformed as the ministers of righteousness; whose end shall be according to their works," (2 Corinthians 11:13-15).

Notice that Paul tells us that Satan is able to **transform** himself into an angel of **light**. His ministers can **transform** themselves into ministers of **righteousness**. Now obviously, Paul is referencing not only fallen angels and Nephilim demons, but also those *pastors* and *teachers* in *his* day who preached a false gospel. Motivated by the legions of the underworld,

197

these preachers and teachers are often remarkable at presenting a false gospel in such a way that the hearers often fail to see through their duplicitousness to the dangerous message *behind* the falsity.

The plain fact of the matter is that today is no different from Paul's day. Many churches (and too many of them are *super* or *mega* churches in size), have pastors and teachers promoting the error resident within the Emergent Church. By following its tenets, people who may start out wanting to worship the one, true God, wind up being deceived into worshiping themselves and ultimately, Satan.

Pulling Them Away

We know that the main thing Satan is after is pulling people *away* from God. To that end, he has created some very complex *schemes*, designed to meet the needs of all types of people. Some become convinced that they have nothing to worry about, because God does not exist. For others, he teaches them that the path to God is found *within*. Still others are taught that it does not matter *what* path a person takes in life, as long as it is *moral* in some relative way, because all paths eventually lead to God. This is what he is out to accomplish. He does not care if a person worships him *directly*, as those do who readily admit or brag that they are Satanists, or witches.

Satan is very happy if he can simply *keep* human beings from *worshiping the God of the Bible*. He does this by polluting their minds with lie after lie, telling their itching ears what they want to hear. In doing so, he has *won* their soul and they do not need to worship him for that to happen. All they need to do is *reject* the truth of *who* Jesus Christ is and *what* He accomplished on Calvary's cross until they die. That is all they need to do, and he has them, because by *default*, if they are *not* worshiping the God of the Bible, they are worshiping *Satan*.

We Are Like Computers

People are like computers. When you turn on a computer, it boots up and then allows you to open a word processing document, for instance. Once the document opens, there are things like the font, font size, and font

People are Like Computers

©2010 F. DERUVO

Only God Can Change Your Defaults!

Both come with a default. For the computer the operating system demands that certain fonts and settings will be automatic.

For the human, our "operating system" (our sin nature) also demands that certain outlooks and attitudes will be automatic.

Because neither system is perfect, breakdowns and problems occur. Fortunately for both - the computer and the human - those defaults can be changed.

styles are in view *by default*. These settings can be manually changed or set so that a different font automatically opens up with the program.

People are born into this world with a sin nature. Because of that sin nature, we are unrighteous *by default*. Only the salvation made available through Jesus Christ has the power to change our *default* setting, from unrighteous to righteous.

As long as people continue to *reject God*, they are worshiping Satan *by default*. This default setting stays like this until such a time as we receive salvation and then it is changed *permanently* and *forever* to one of righteousness. The process of retraining ourselves in God's strength to understand and apply these new defaults takes a lifetime.

People who are born into this world with a sin nature (all of us), and continue to reject the truth of the Gospel are open to all manner of suggestions and delusions simply because they have no absolute truth by which they can hang their hat (or soul, in this case). In rejecting that truth, they are open to any form of what is *stated* to be truth, because they also learn to go by their *emotions*. Since our emotions are corrupt, as our flesh is corrupt due to the sin nature, we *cannot* rely on these to support us in our search for the truth. Too many people do though, and even as Christians, we tend to rely too much on emotions, instead of the truth of God's Word (whether we *feel* like His Word is true, or not). For every unique person, Satan constructs a *unique* truth, and of course, every truth he creates is merely another version of his main *lie*.

In 2010, we are hearing and seeing more and more things at work in the skies over our planet, in our churches, in our books, in our music, and all of it intends to turn us *from* God *to* Satan. As Satan continues to work in this decade and future decades (up to the time decreed by God that human history will end), we are guaranteed that we will see more alien and paranormal activity. It will become more spectacular and frequent.

More and more people will see a glimpse behind the dimensional curtain as time moves onward. Unfortunately, what they see will be far different from the reality that *actually* exists. Yet, this is all part of the delusion that God is sending, so that the citizens of this earth will believe the lie; the lie that says we are gods. We are *not* gods. We are created human beings and we owe our allegiance and worship to the God of the universe – Creator - not to some wannabe pretender to the throne!

As we move toward the culmination of all things, we must be ever vigilant, and *remain* in fellowship with our Lord and Savior. This is the only thing that guarantees our ability to *overcome*. Failure to do so does *not* mean we lose salvation. It means we are out of fellowship and open to the suggestions and deceptions of the enemy. Satan wants Christians to quarrel over this doctrine or that doctrine. He wants us to become so involved in disputes that we have no time to fulfill our true calling; the Great Commission.

God Wants All We Are And All We Possess
God wants *all* that we are and all that we possess, in order that He might live His life in and through us. He wants us to be able to glorify Him because He knows that this is why we were *originally created*, and because of that, we are not whole until we do. We *need* to be able to live in such a way that God is glorified in all things. We *need* to exercise faith in order that His Name will receive honor.

As Christians, we need to wake up to the fact that all around us, people are being drawn into the End Times deception. It is a deception that ends in eternal death; their eternal death. Brothers and sisters in the Lord, we must acknowledge that without God, we are nothing. Without Him, we can *do* nothing.

Many people say that the End Times deception involves a wrong view of the Rapture. How sad is *that*? The End Times deception is merely the exact same deception that Satan sprang on Eve. Because she chose to listen to the Tempter, and agreed with her *emotions*, she gave into his temptation. This resultant spiritual death has passed onto all of us.

The End Times deception is one in which Satan has created this multi-faceted scheme of bringing all people together to believe the simple untruth, that all humanity is *god*. Eve believed it when he told her that her eyes would be open and she would become *like* God. Her emotions heard that and grabbed for it!

The End Times delusion has *nothing* to do with Eschatology and everything to do with *Christology* (study of Christ) and *Soteriology* (study of salvation). Hasn't Satan created a cesspool of confusion and doubt so that even Christians have taken up his cause by turning one against another.

Matthew 24:9-10 states, "*Then shall they deliver you up to be afflicted, and shall kill you: and ye shall be hated of all nations for my name's sake. And then shall many be offended, and shall betray one another, and shall hate one another.*"

2 Timothy 3:1-5 states, "*This know also, that in the last days perilous times shall come. For men shall be lovers of their own selves, covetous, boasters, proud, blasphemers, disobedient to parents, unthankful, unholy, Without natural affection, trucebreakers, false accusers, incontinent, fierce, despisers of those that are good, Traitors, heady, highminded, lovers of pleasures more than lovers of God; Having a form of godliness, but denying the power thereof: from such turn away.*"

We Must Be About the Master's Business
It certainly seems clear that there will be division in the visible Church, because as it becomes much more difficult to remain a Christian *in public*, more and more of the professing Christians will find churches that teach what they want to hear. Tolerance for same-sex marriage, abortion and a myriad of other things will separate the sheep from the goats.

Beyond this, we know that divisions over non-essential doctrines have and will continue to cause rifts, not only in churches, but also between *authentic* Christians. No, we all need to be like R. C. Chapman, who lived from 1803 to 1902. He refused to allow any Eschatological differences between his fellow Christians separate them from the main task. That task, never rescinded, is the Great Commission.

In this period of last days, we must avoid being caught up in arguments and quarrels. We must be aware of what Satan is doing and regardless of what we believe about aliens and Nephilim, we *must* warn people about the delusion and deception that is already here and growing. We must warn them whether they listen or not. We must pray to God that He *will* open their ears that they may listen to *the* truth.

Resources for Your Library

BOOKS:

- Agape Leadership (R. C. Chapman), by Peterson & Strauch
- Alien Encounters, by Chuck Missler
- The Alien Interviews, by L. A. Marzulli
- The Anti-Supernatural Bias of "Ex-Christians," by Fred DeRuvo
- The Church in Prophecy, by John F. Walvoord
- Confrontations, by Jacques Vallee
- Dictionary of Premillennial Theology, Mal Couch, Editor
- Dispensationalism Tomorrow & Beyond, by Christopher Cone, Ed.
- Earth's Earliest Ages, by G. H. Pember
- Exploring the Future, by John Phillips
- Fallen Angels, the Watchers and the Origins of Evil - Lumpkin
- Footsteps of the Messiah, by Arnold G. Fruchtenbaum
- Future Israel (Why Christian Anti-Judaism Must Be Challenged), by E. Ray Clendenen, Ed.
- Giants on the Earth, by Timothy Green Beckley
- Israelology, by Arnold G. Fruchtenbaum
- The Lost Book of Enoch, Transliteration by Joseph B. Lumpkin
- The Moody Handbook of Theology, by Paul Enns
- The Mountains of Israel, by Norma Archbold
- The Nephilim, by Patrick Heron
- Nephilim Stargates, by Thomas R. Horn
- The Pre-Wrath Rapture Answered, by Lee W. Brainard
- Pursuit of Holiness, by Jerry Bridges
- Things to Come, by J. Dwight Pentecost
- UFO End-Time Delusion, by David A. Lewis & Robert Shreckwise
- What on Earth is God Doing? By Renald Showers

Resources for Your Library (cont'd)

INTERNET:

- Anti-Preterist Blog   antipreterist.wordpress.com
- Ariel Ministries   www.ariel.org
- Berean Watchmen   www.bereanwatchmen.com
- Foothill Bible Church   www.foothill-bible.org
- Friends of Israel   www.foi.org
- Grace to You   www.gty.org
- Prophezine   www.prophezine.com
- Prophecy in the News   www.prophecyinthenews.com
- Study-Grow-Know   www.studygrowknow.com
- Study-Grow-Know Blog   www.modres.wordpress.com
- Tyndale Theological Seminary   www.tyndale.edu

Find more of Fred DeRuvo's books at the following places:

- Prophecy in the News   www.prophecyinthenews.com
- Study-Grow-Know   www.studygrowknow.com
- Amazon   www.amazon.com
- CreateSpace   www.createspace.com

4794446R0

Made in the USA
Charleston, SC
17 March 2010